Easy See, Easy Stitch
Cross Stitch

B.J. McDonald

©2004 by BJ McDonald

Published by

An imprint of F+W Publications, Inc.

700 East State Street • Iola, WI 54990-0001
715-445-2214 • 888-457-2873
www.krause.com

Our toll-free number to place an order or obtain
a free catalog is (800) 258-0929.

Library of Congress Catalog Number: 2004093861
ISBN: 0-87349-766-X
Edited by Maria L. Turner
Designed by Donna Mummery
Printed in China

Acknowledgments

Once again, designers Phyllis Dobbs, Pam Kellogg, Roberta Madeleine, and Mike Vickery did their magic in creating spectacular designs. Designer Anne Stanton did the clear, concise stitch diagrams. Thank you, designers: You're the greatest.

A special appreciation to Adam Original for producing exciting, new prefinished products just for this book. Without the support of Adam Original, Charles Craft, Coats & Clark, DMC, Krause, Kreinik, and Zweigart, this book wouldn't have been possible. So a big thank you to all of the supporting companies.

Thank you, Ron Whitfield, for your patience and superb photography; to my uncle, LD Sharp, for making his home available for photo sessions; and to my daughter Iva McDonald, Sandra Thomas, and baby Abigail Sharp for modeling.

Thank you my dear friend Julie Stephani for your guidance and encouragement. Special recognition and thanks to page designer Donna Mummery, cover designer Mary Lou Marshall, and my editor Maria Turner for making the finished product fantastic.

Preface

When we talk about "easy see, easy stitch cross stitch," we're talking about using smaller-count fabrics to create projects that are just as beautiful as those designed for larger-count fabrics. All the wonderful projects in this book were made this way. Discover how these fabrics are so much easier to see and quicker to stitch.

7-Count

8-Count

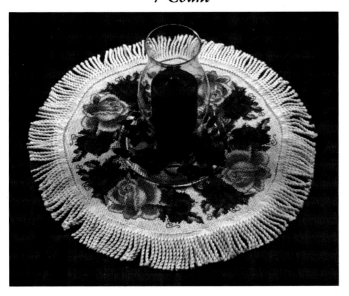

10-Count

11-Count

Table of Contents

Acknowledgments 3

Preface 3

Introduction 6

Easy See, Easy Stitch Fabrics 8

Easy See, Easy Stitch for
Anniversaries and Weddings................................. 10
- 50th Wedding Anniversary Table Topper 11
- 25th Wedding Anniversary Table Topper 14
- Ring Bearer Pillow and Bridal Purse Set 15
- Wedding Table Topper 18

Easy See, Easy Stitch for Babies............................. 22
- Bear Family Afghan 23
- Butterfly Bib and Burp Towel Set............................. 26
- Birth Announcement Sampler 29

Easy See, Easy Stitch for Christmas 32
- Moose Stocking 33
- Ornament Stocking and Ornaments 36
- Festive Bear Vest 39
- Ornament Tree Skirt 41
- Poinsettia Table Topper 44

Easy See, Easy Stitch for Décor and More ... 48
- Daisy Pillow Sham 49
- Daisy Checkbook Cover....................................... 54
- Four Seasons Candle Doilies 55
- Rejoice in the Lord Framed Piece............................. 64
- Lace Border Table Toppers 67
- Rhode Island Red Rooster and Buff Orpington Hen
  Pillow Shams and Framed Pieces.............................. 70
- Grape Cottage Huck Towel 80
- Gooseberry Cottage Huck Towel 82
- Cherry Cottage Huck Towel 84
- Four Seasons Coasters 86
- Teatime Tea Tray... 88
- Our Family Memories Album Cover 90
- Victorian Alphabet Sampler 93

Easy See, Easy Stitch Friendship 96
* Flowers in the Garden of Life
  Afghan and Framed Verse 97
* The Path Sampler 110

Easy See, Easy Stitch
for Special Events 112
* Happy Birthday Table Topper 113
* Graduation Sampler 116
* Halloween Bear Table Topper 119

Easy See, Easy Stitch Wearables.........121
* Hawaiian Floral Shawl................................122
* Morning Glory Vests.................................125
* Monogrammed Winter Scarf..........................128
* Rose Monogrammed Shirt 131

General Instructions 132
* Fabrics 132
* Needles 132
* Threads 133
* Determining Finished Size 135
* Centering a Design 135
* Cleaning a Stitched Piece............................135
* Treating Stains....................................135
* Storing a Stitched Piece 135
* Basic Guidelines of Counted Cross Stitch 135
* Charts 136
* Working with Waste Canvas.........................137
* Stitch Diagrams 137

Needlework Accessories 139

Embroidery Floss Conversion Chart 142

Resources 143

Contributing Designers.....................144

B.J. McDonald

Introduction

I was first introduced to what I call "easy see, easy stitch" (smaller-count) fabrics back in the '80s. These fabrics have fewer stitches per inch and include 6-, 7-, 8-, 10-, and 11-count fabrics. They are much easier to stitch because the fabric holes are easier to see. They are wonderful to stitch on for anyone who has less-than-perfect eyesight or has tired eyes. The fabrics also work up more quickly for stitchers who are on-the-go. I have always included charts with larger symbols, so the charts are easier to read as well.

Below are examples of two of the easy see, easy stitch fabrics. Notice how the design shown stitched on 6-count is much larger than the same design stitched on the 11-count. Designs will gradually get smaller with each larger fabric count size. The chart for the heart design is on page 136.

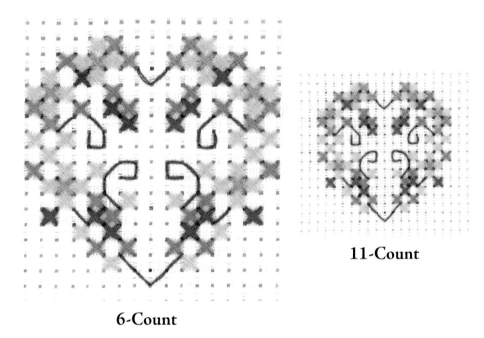

11-Count

6-Count

It has been my passion over the years to present beautiful designs for stitchers using these smaller-count fabrics. The higher fabric counts—14, 16, 18, 28, 32, 36, etc.—have more threads (squares) per inch and are more difficult to see and stitch. For years, many stitchers and designers thought the smaller-count fabrics were only for simple designs for beginners or were for elementary designs for children. I have worked with designers and have encouraged them to create elegant designs that anyone would be proud to use as home décor accents or to give as gifts.

Throughout the years, the selections within this fabric group have grown to include more sophisticated fabrics to choose from. In addition to cotton, damask, and wool Aidas, there are Country Aida, Klostern, Tilla, Tula, Herta, Monk's Cloth, Merino, damasks in various styles, and wool Hardanger. Then came the smaller-count prefinished items to stitch on: baby bibs; cottage huck towels; ring bearer's pillows; purses; album and checkbook covers; tree skirts; pillow shams; stockings; and vests. Next, a very impressive list of items was added, including prefinished table runners, napkins, and table toppers with an equally impressive palette of colors.

I still stitch on linens and other higher-count fabrics, but I like to have an ongoing project on the easy see, easy stitch fabrics to give my eyes a rest. There usually are fewer or no fractional stitches in designs for these fabrics, which also speeds up stitching.

Quicker projects and easier-to-see fabrics and charts: What welcome choices for today's stitchers. Most of us lead busy lives. We have less leisure time. When we take time for stitching, we want to make the best of it and enjoy ourselves in the process.

We live in the technical age where everything seems to revolve around computers. More people work on computers all day and also have computers in their homes. Our eyes are tired after a day of over-use. It's refreshing to stitch on these easy see, easy stitch fabrics, even after a day's work on the computer.

Numerous times I've heard former stitchers make the remark, "I used to cross-stitch but stopped because I couldn't see the fabrics anymore. With these easy see, easy stitch fabrics, I can see how to stitch again."

Easy see, easy stitch fabrics are fun to stitch. That alone reduces stress. Cross-stitch is for enjoyment, and easy see, easy stitch fabrics can certainly increase the pleasure you find from stitching.

As a cross-stitcher, you already know how therapeutic cross-stitch is. When you focus your attention on a stitching project, stress lessens with each stitch you make. Some say it's the repetitiveness of stitch after stitch. Others say it's seeing a blank piece of fabric become a picture—a masterpiece created with needle and thread. I believe, like many others, that it is the combination of these things that have a calming and relaxing effect.

Try playing music while you are stitching. Music has been proven to be a great therapy. It can calm and elevate your mood, counteract anxiety and depression, and even lessen muscle tension for easier relaxation. The next time you sit down to stitch, try listening to your favorite CD while you stitch. Determine for yourself if cross-stitch and soothing music make a great stress-reducing combination. I personally love listening to Enya, light classical (my absolute favorite is Fur Elise), blues, jazz, and sometimes, when I really feel spunky, it's rock 'n' roll. Choose music that calms and relaxes you. For some it will be classical, others jazz, country, rock 'n' roll, etc.

Now is the time to settle down in a comfortable place with good lighting, play your favorite CD, and experience the joy of stitching on easy see, easy stitch fabrics.

Happy stitching,

Bj. McDonald

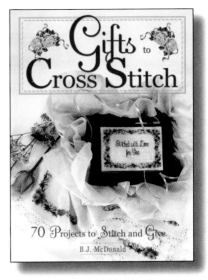

Gifts to Cross Stitch, also authored by B.J. McDonald and published in 2003 by Krause Publications, features 70 projects to stitch and give.

Easy See, Easy Stitch Fabrics

The first group of fabrics, below on this page and continuing straight across to the facing page, shows how the finished design size changes as you work from a 6-count through an 11-count fabric.

6-Count
Herta (z)

7-Count
Klostern (z)

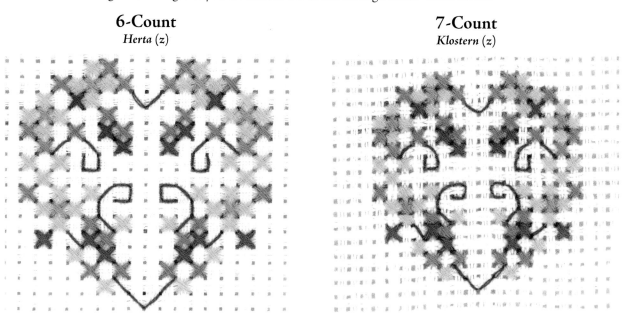

Manufacturers are listed by a code after the fabric's name, along with the colors available in that particular fabric. Fabric name in parenthesis is the actual fabric sample shown. There are more fabrics within these categories, as shown on this page and the next.

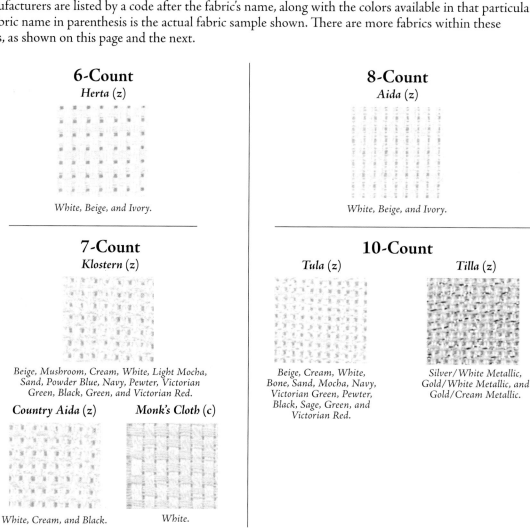

6-Count
Herta (z)

White, Beige, and Ivory.

8-Count
Aida (z)

White, Beige, and Ivory.

7-Count
Klostern (z)

Beige, Mushroom, Cream, White, Light Mocha, Sand, Powder Blue, Navy, Pewter, Victorian Green, Black, Green, and Victorian Red.

Country Aida (z)

Monk's Cloth (c)

White, Cream, and Black.

White.

10-Count
Tula (z)

Tilla (z)

Beige, Cream, White, Bone, Sand, Mocha, Navy, Victorian Green, Pewter, Black, Sage, Green, and Victorian Red.

Silver/White Metallic, Gold/White Metallic, and Gold/Cream Metallic.

8-Count
Aida (z)

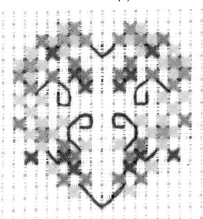

10-Count
Tula (z)

11-Count
Aida (z)

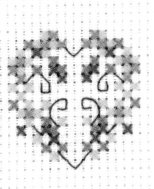

Cotton Aida (z)

White, Beige, Black,
Antique White, Ivory,
Light Blue, Navy,
Yellow, Christmas
Green, Pink, and
Christmas Red.

11-Count
Cotton Aida (c)

Antique White, Ivory,
and White.

Cotton Aida (d)

White and Ecru.

*Damask Aida
(in Patterned Weaves) (z)*

Schonfels Damask: White
and Eggshell; Bundle of Bows:
White, Eggshell, Ash Rose,
and Wedgwood; Dacapo:
White and Eggshell; and Viale
Damask: White and Eggshell.

Wool Aida (z)

White and Antique White.

Merino Afghan (z)

Antique White.

Fabric Manufacturers

(c) Charles Craft, Inc.

(d) The DMC® Corporation

(z) Zweigart® THE needlework fabric

Easy See, Easy Stitch for

Anniversaries and Weddings

Cross Stitch: 3 strands

Backstitch: 2 strands

Stitch Count: 128 wide x 86 high

Approximate Finished Size (10-count):

12⅞" x 8⅝"

Supplies

- Zweigart® Prefinished Gold/Cream 10-count Rondo Table Topper
- DMC® 6-Strand Embroidery Floss
  - 1 skein each #319, #367, #368, #369, #725, #781, #972
  - 2 skeins #783
- 1 skein DMC® #5282 6-Strand Metallic Floss
- #24 Tapestry Needle

50th Wedding Anniversary Table Topper

Design by Phyllis Dobbs
Stitching by Kay Freeman

Commemorate those special golden wedding anniversaries with custom prefinished table toppers. This project was stitched on a gold/cream Rondo topper, embellished with gold metallic.

DMC® 6-Strand Embroidery Floss

▲ 367 Pistachio Green, dark
○ 368 Pistachio Green, light
╱ 369 Pistachio Green, very light
╲ 725 Topaz
● 783 Topaz, medium

Blended Needle

(two strands metallic and one strand regular floss)

✚ 5282 Gold DMC® 6-Strand Metallic Floss and
972 Canary, deep, DMC® 6-Strand Embroidery Floss

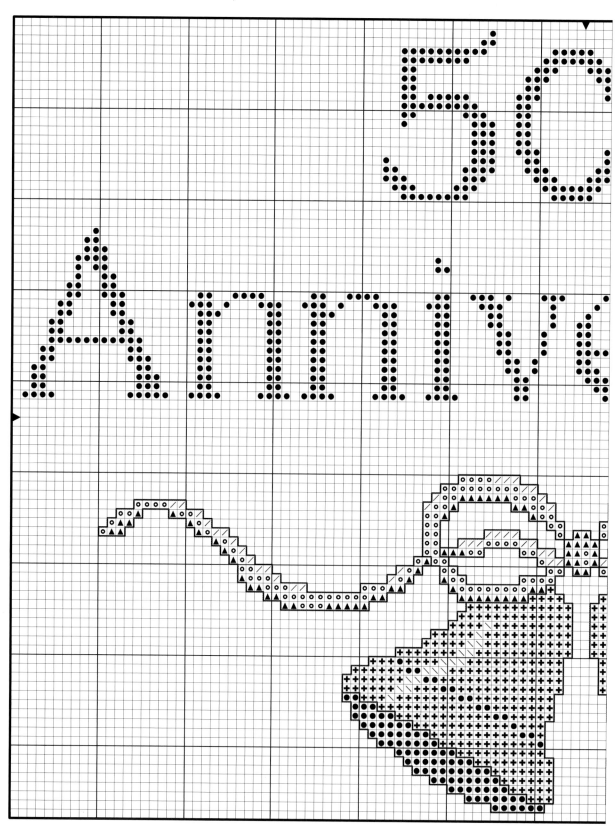

Backstitch Instructions

Bell: DMC® 781 Topaz, dark.
Bow: DMC® 319 Pistachio Green, very dark.

25th Wedding Anniversary Table Topper

Design by Phyllis Dobbs
Stitching by Kay Freeman

A variation of the previous project, this table topper celebrates a silver anniversary. It was stitched on a white Rondo topper, embellished with silver metallic.

General Instructions

You will use the same chart that was used for the 50th anniversary table topper, except with symbol and color changes.

DMC® 6-Strand Embroidery Floss

▲	367	Pistachio Green, dark
○	368	Pistachio Green, light
/	369	Pistachio Green, very light
●	414	Steel Gray, dark (bell)
■	415	Pearl Gray ("25th")
•	415	Pearl Gray ("Anniversary")
\	762	Pearl Gray, very light

Blended Needle

(two strands metallic and one strand regular floss)

✛	5283	Silver DMC® 6-Strand Metallic Floss <u>and</u>
	415	Pearl Gray DMC® 6-Strand Embroidery Floss (bell)

Cross Stitch: 3 strands

Backstitch: 2 strands

Stitch Count: 128 wide x 86 high

Approximate Finished Size (10-count):
12⅞" x 8⅝"

Supplies

- Zweigart® Prefinished White 10-count Rondo Table Topper
- DMC® 6-Strand Embroidery Floss
  - 1 skein each #319, #367, #368, #369, #413, #414, #762
  - 2 skeins #415
- 1 skein DMC® #5283 6-Strand Metallic Floss
- #24 Tapestry Needle

Backstitch Instructions

Bell: DMC® 413 Pewter Gray, dark.
Bow: DMC® 319 Pistachio Green, very dark.

tip

For the silver anniversary table topper, the "25th" and "Anniversary" will be in DMC 415 Pearl Gray. The chart on the previous page shows a dot symbol, which represents a different color.

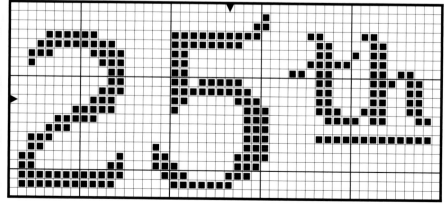

Ring Bearer Pillow
and Bridal Purse Set

Designs by Phyllis Dobbs

The wedding ensemble will be complete with this luxurious damask pillow and purse set. The ring bearer pillow and bridal purse are exquisite prefinished items made with 11-count cream Schonfels damask with a 3" floral-lace trim. Dainty pink rosettes and pearls give an additional elegance to the floral pattern woven within the damask fabric. You'll love how quick and easy these projects are to stitch, and the participants will love these mementos from the wedding. The purse can be used in years to come for attending other after-five events.

Cross Stitch: 3 strands
Stitch Count: 33 wide x 33 high
**Approximate Finished Size
(10-count):** 3¼" circle

Supplies

- Beautiful Accents™ Prefinished
  Ring Bearer's Pillow made with
  Zweigart® 11-count
  Cream Schonfels Damask
- DMC® 6-Strand Embroidery Floss
  - 1 skein each #320, #604, and
    Ecru (optional)
- 20 4mm Round Ivory
  Simulated Pearls
- 5 Offray® ⅓" Pink
  Ribbon Rosettes
- Cream Sewing Thread or Ecru
  6-Strand Embroidery Floss
- #24 Tapestry Needle

Ring Bearer Pillow

General Instructions

Attach pearls with cream sewing thread or ecru 6-strand embroidery floss. Sew a ⅓"-wide light pink rose in the center square of pillow. Sew the remaining four roses centered in the open areas around the edge of the design. Refer to photograph for additional assistance.

DMC® 6-Strand Embroidery Floss

✖ 320   Pistachio Green, medium
☐ 604   Cranberry, light

4mm Pearls

●   Ivory Pearls

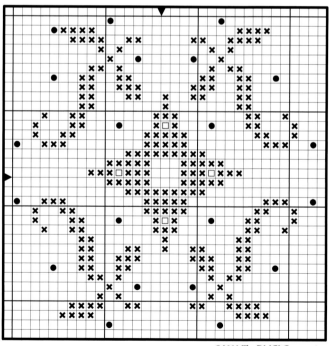

Cross Stitch: 3 strands
Stitch Count: 33 wide x 33 high
Approximate Finished Size
   (10-count): 3¼" circle

Supplies

- Beautiful Accents™ Prefinished
  Bride's Purse made with
  Zweigart® 11-count Cream
  Schonfels Damask
- DMC® 6-Strand Embroidery Floss
  - 1 skein each #320, #604, and
    Ecru (optional)
- 25 4mm Round Ivory
  Simulated Pearls
- 4 Offray® ⅓" Pink
  Ribbon Rosettes
- Cream Sewing Thread or
  Ecru 6-Strand Embroidery Floss
- #24 Tapestry Needle

Bride's Purse

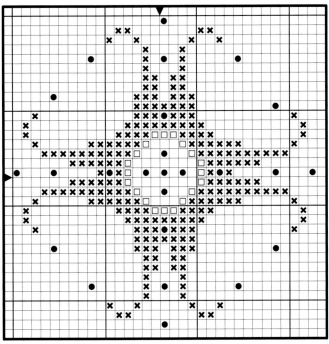

©2003 The DMC® Corporation

General Instructions

Attach pearls with cream sewing thread or ecru 6-strand embroidery floss. Sew a ⅓"-wide light pink rose in the center of each of the open curves. Refer to the project photograph for additional assistance, if necessary.

DMC® 6-Strand Embroidery Floss

✖	320	Pistachio Green, medium
☐	604	Cranberry, light

4mm Pearls

●	Ivory Pearls

Cross Stitch: 3 strands

Backstitch: 2 strands

Stitch Count: 127 wide x 107 high

Approximate Finished Size (10-count): 12¾" x 10¾"

Supplies

- Zweigart® Prefinished 10-count Seafoam Green Rondo Table Topper
- DMC® 6-Strand Embroidery Floss
  - 1 skein each #319, #368, #369, #600, #605, #3805, #3806
  - 2 skeins #367
- #26 Tapestry Needle

Wedding Table Topper

Design by Phyllis Dobbs
Stitching by Kay Freeman

Both the bride and the groom will love this wedding table topper commemorating their special occasion. Use the table topper as a special setting for the couple at the reception or as a setting for the cake and gifts—or both! It's a beautiful keepsake of this joyous union of marriage, a keepsake that can be used for each anniversary.

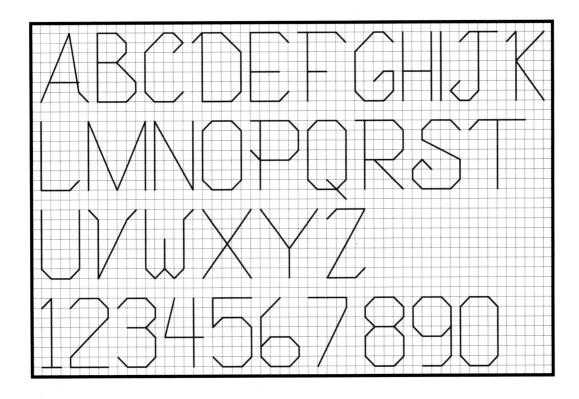

DMC® 6-Strand Embroidery Floss

▲	367	Pistachio Green, dark		□	605	Cranberry, very light
○	368	Pistachio Green, light		●	3805	Cranberry, dark
/	369	Pistachio Green, very light		+	3806	Cyclamen Pink, light

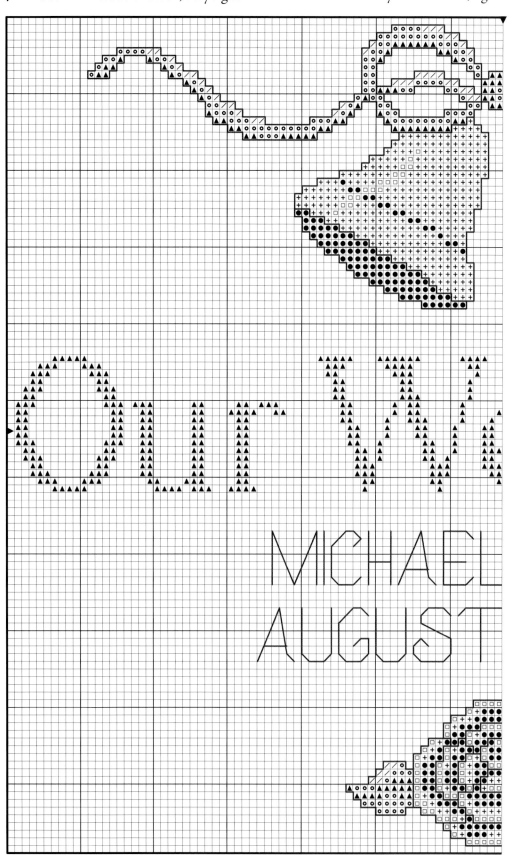

Backstitch Instructions

Bell and rose: DMC® 600 Watermelon.

Leaves and bow: DMC® 319 Pistachio Green, very dark.

Names and date: DMC® 367 Pistachio Green, dark.

Easy See, Easy Stitch for
Babies

Cross Stitch: 6 strands
Backstitch: 2 strands
Balloon Strings: 4 strands
French Knots: 3 strands wrapped three times
Stitch Count: 116 wide x 98 high
Approximate Finished Size (7-count): 16½" x 14"

Supplies

- 42" square Charles Craft 7-count White Monk's Cloth
- DMC® 6-Strand Embroidery Floss
  - 1 skein each White, #300, #301, #310, #322, #605, #676, #729, #744, #891, #893, #894, #912, #913, #921, #938, #955, #3078, #3325, #3776
- #22 Tapestry Needle

Bear Family Afghan

Papa Bear, Mama Bear, and Baby Bear won't be the only ones with smiles for this luxuriously soft Monk's Cloth afghan. Baby will love the cuddly softness, and you'll enjoy stitching on this easy see, easy stitch 7-count fabric. A baby's afghan is a wonderful keepsake to be enjoyed for generations.

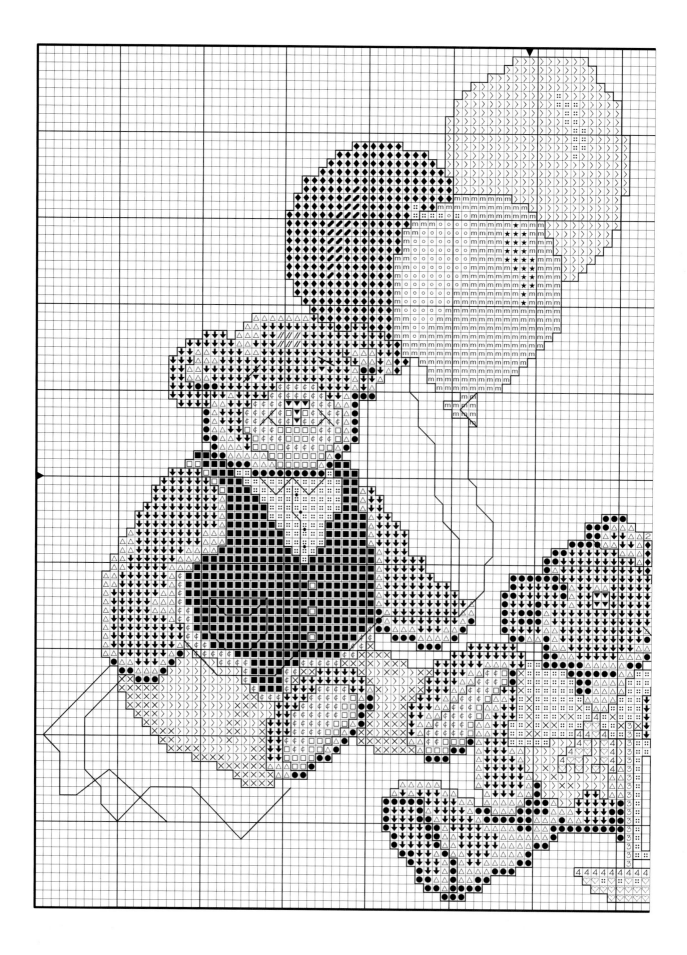

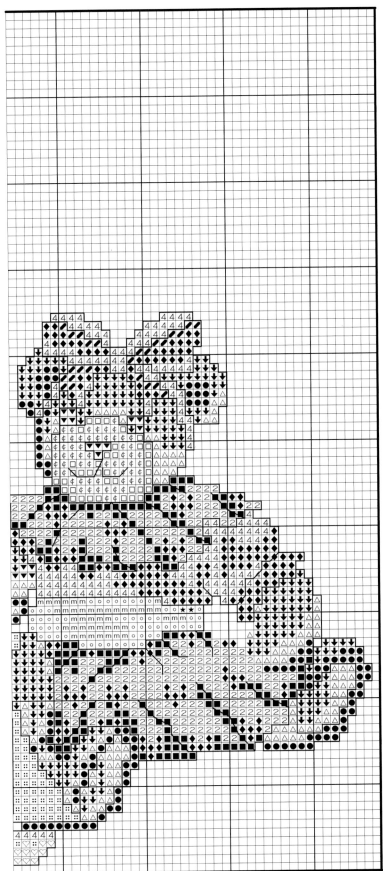

DMC® 6-Strand Embroidery Floss

::	White	White
●	300	Mahogany, very dark
△	301	Mahogany, medium
3	310	Black
✕	322	Navy Blue, very light
⬤	605	Cranberry, very light
¢	676	Old Gold, light
□	729	Old Gold, medium
■	744	Yellow, pale
♡	891	Carnation, dark
4	893	Carnation, light
◆	894	Carnation, very light
o	912	Emerald Green, light
m	913	Nile Green, medium
//	921	Copper
▼	938	Coffee Brown, ultra dark
★	955	Nile Green, light
2	3078	Golden Yellow, very light
⟩	3325	Baby Blue, light
↓	3776	Mahogany, light

Backstitch Instructions

Pink balloon: DMC® 893 Carnation, light.
Green balloon: DMC® 912 Emerald Green, light.
Blue balloon: DMC® 322 Navy Blue, very light.
Strings: DMC® 891 Carnation, dark.
Sailboat: DMC® 893 Carnation, light.
Sailboat helm: DMC® 310 Black.
Baby Bear's clothing, neck of Papa Bear's vest, and Papa Bear's pants: DMC® 322 Navy Blue, very light.
Bow: DMC® 893 Carnation, light.
Vest and dress: DMC® 3776 Mahogany, light.
All other backstitch: DMC® 300 Mahogany, very dark.

French Knots

• Papa Bear's vest: DMC® 322 Navy Blue, very light.

For a lighter texture, cross stitch with four strands, backstitch with two strands, and stitch the balloon strings with two strands. Experiment on an outer section of the fabric to determine which texture you prefer.

Cross Stitch: 4 strands

Backstitch: 2 strands

Stitch Count: 71 wide x 22 high

Approximate Finished Size

(8-count): 8⅞" x 2¾"

Supplies

- Zweigart® Cottage Huck Bib
  with 8-count Aida Insert
  (white bib with pistachio borders)
- DMC® 6-Strand Embroidery Floss
  - 1 skein each #310, #317, #413,
    #414, #564, #727, #800, #961,
    #962, #963, #3716, #3799, #3838,
    #3839, #3840
- #22 Tapestry Needle

Butterfly Bib and Burp Towel Set

Designs by Pamela Kellogg
Stitching by Kim Dennett

Baby never had it so good! This butterfly bib and burp towel set looks time-consuming, but the 8-count cottage huck fabric fills quickly with stitches. Encased within a pistachio floral border, butterflies dance around colorful delicate blue and pink flowers. In the center of the design is a heart shape with "Baby" inscribed within—a heart for love, as baby and new parents will love this precious set.

DMC® 6-Strand Embroidery Floss

■	310	Black	¢	962	Dusty Rose, medium
Z	317	Pewter Gray	2	963	Dusty Rose, ultra very light
✗	413	Pewter Gray, dark	🌙	3716	Dusty Rose, very light
✦	414	Steel Gray, dark	♡	3799	Pewter Gray, very dark
★	564	Jade, very light	♥	3838	Lavender Blue, dark
4	727	Topaz, very light	☆	3839	Lavender Blue, medium
m	800	Delft Blue, pale	➔	3840	Lavender Blue, light
✖	961	Dusty Rose, dark			

Bib

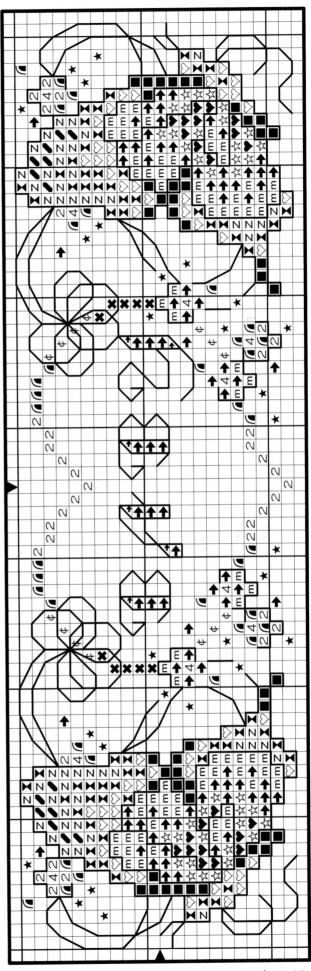

Backstitch Instructions

Butterfly: DMC® 310 Black.

Ribbon: DMC® 727 Topaz, very light.

Pink flowers: DMC® 962 Dusty Rose, medium.

"Baby": DMC® 3838 Lavender Blue, dark.

Blue flowers: DMC® 3839 Lavender Blue, medium.

The design fits very close on the bib. Before stitching, count stitches in bib and in chart to find center and to reconfirm that complete design fits within the bib.

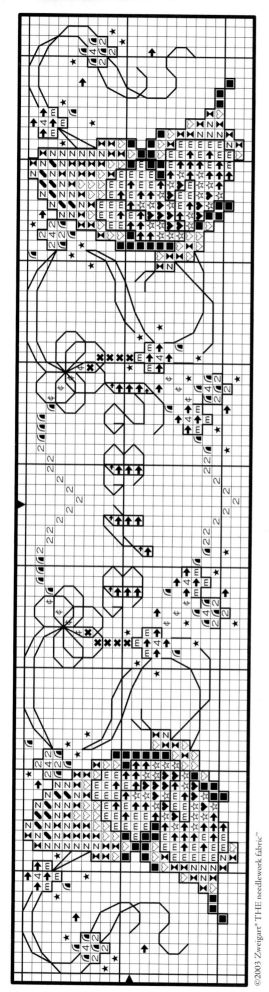

Cross Stitch: 4 strands
Backstitch: 2 strands
Stitch Count: 93 wide x 22 high
Approximate Finished Size (8-count): 11⅝" x 2¾"

Supplies

- Zweigart® Cottage Huck Towel with 8-count Aida insert (white towel with pistachio borders)
- DMC® 6-Strand Embroidery Floss
  - 1 skein each #310, #317, #413, #414, #564, #727, #800, #961, #962, #963, #3716, #3799, #3838, #3839, 3840
- #22 Tapestry Needle

Burp Towel

DMC® 6-Strand Embroidery Floss

■	310	Black	¢	962	Dusty Rose, medium
Z	317	Pewter Gray	2	963	Dusty Rose, ultra very light
✗	413	Pewter Gray, dark			
◖	414	Steel Gray, dark	◖	3716	Dusty Rose, very light
★	564	Jade, very light	♡	3799	Pewter Gray, very dark
4	727	Topaz, very light	♥	3838	Lavender Blue, dark
m	800	Delft Blue, pale	☆	3839	Lavender Blue, medium
✗	961	Dusty Rose, dark	➜	3840	Lavender Blue, light

Backstitch Instructions

Butterfly: DMC® 310 Black.
Ribbon: DMC® 727 Topaz, very light.
Pink flowers: DMC® 962 Dusty Rose, medium.
"Baby": DMC® 3838 Lavender Blue, dark.
Blue flowers: DMC® 3839 Lavender Blue, medium.

tip

The design fits very close on the towel. Before stitching, count the stitches in the towel and in the chart to find the center and to reconfirm that the complete design fits within the towel.

Cross Stitch: 3 strands
Backstitch: 2 strands
French Knots: 2 strands
wrapped three times
Stitch Count: 78 wide x 98 high
Approximate Finished Size (11-count):
7¹⁄₈" x 9"

Supplies

- DMC® 11-count White Aida
- DMC® 6-Strand Embroidery Floss
  - 1 skein each #340, #420, #543, #563, #564, #727, #745, #746, #761, #800, #809, #839, #841, #842, #912, #954, #3046, #3713, #3823, Ecru
- #24 Tapestry Needle
- 7½" x 9½" Wood Frame

Birth Announcement Sampler

Design by Roberta Madeleine
Stitching by Lois Hiles

A birth announcement sampler is a wonderful keepsake recording of pertinent information of the new baby. This sampler is appropriate for boys and girls with a simple change in floss color for the baby's name.

DMC® 6-Strand Embroidery Floss

V	340	Blue Violet, medium
╱	420	Hazelnut Brown, dark
+	543	Beige Brown, ultra very light
♡	563	Jade, light
△	564	Jade, very light
☆	727	Topaz, very light
I	745	Light Yellow, pale
∧	746	Off-White
◢	761	Salmon, light
T	800	Delft Blue, pale
□	809	Delft Blue
♥	839	Beige Brown, dark
⊥	841	Beige Brown, light
Z	842	Beige Brown, very light
O	912	Emerald Green, light
L	954	Nile Green
—	3046	Yellow Beige, medium
♠	3713	Salmon, very light
X	3823	Yellow, ultra pale
4	Ecru	Ecru

Backstitch Instructions

Girl's name: DMC® 221 Shell Pink, medium dark.

Boy's name: DMC® 517 Wedgwood, medium.

Verse, date, and weight: DMC® 912 Emerald Green, light.

All other backstitch: DMC® 839 Beige Brown, dark.

French Knot Instructions

• Date: DMC® 912 Emerald Green, light.
• Bees: DMC® 839 Beige Brown, dark.

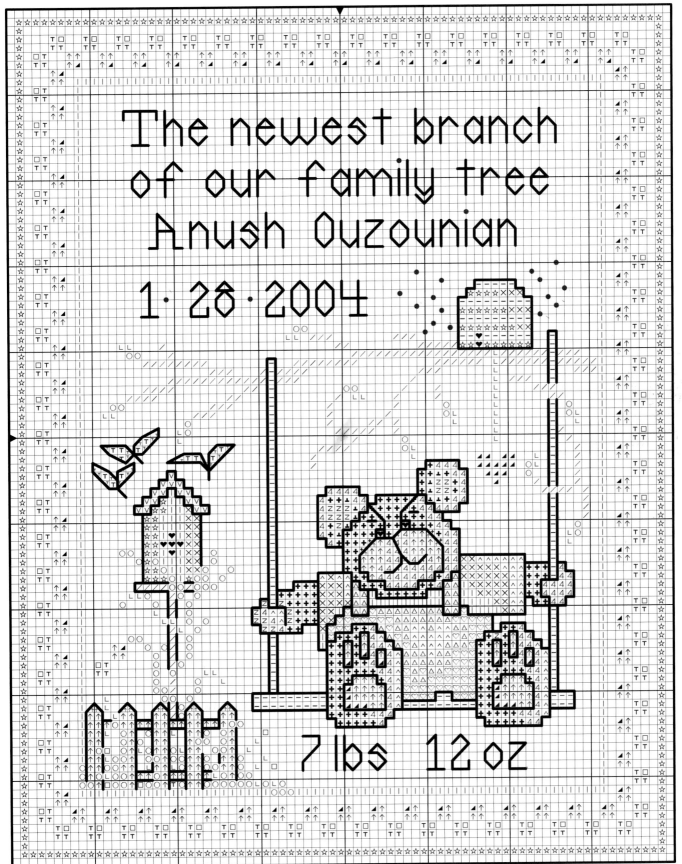

The newest branch
of our family tree
Anush Ouzounian
1·28·2004

7 lbs 12 oz

©2003 The DMC® Corporation

Easy See, Easy Stitch for
Christmas

Cross Stitch: 1 strand
(#3 pearl cotton)
Backstitch: 3 strands (6-strand
embroidery floss)
Stitch Count: 63 wide x 100 high
Approximate Finished Size (7-count):
9" x 14¼"

Supplies
- Adam Original Prefinished Stocking
  made with Zweigart® 7-count
  Sand Klostern
- DMC® #3 Pearl Cotton
  - 1 skein each #310, #319, #367, #368,
    #369, #433, #435, #436, #437,
    #666, #677, #725, #772, #813,
    #839, #840, #841, #842, #898, #912
- DMC® 6-Strand Embroidery Floss
  - 1 skein each #666, #772, #898
- #20 Tapestry Needle
  (#3 pearl cotton or
  6 strands embroidery floss)
- #24 Tapestry Needle
  (3 strands embroidery floss)

Moose Stocking

Design by Mike Vickery

This moose doesn't care that the lights are tangled; he's got the Christmas spirit. Outdoorsmen will love the rustic look of the stocking and moose ... all lit up for Christmas. And you'll love stitching this prefinished 7-count stocking. The stocking has a zipper in the back to pull out the lining when stitching. The stitching goes so fast, you'll want to stitch another one right away.

General Instructions

Refer to accompanying alphabet. Count out the letters and spaces in the name before stitching. Measure four rows down from the top to start stitching the name.

Backstitch Instructions

Use DMC® 6-strand embroidery floss on all backstitch.
Name and line underneath: DMC® 666 Christmas Red, bright.
Light cords: DMC® 772 Yellow Green, very light.
Moose: DMC® 898 Coffee Brown, very dark.

DMC® #3 Pearl Cotton

●	310	Black
♠	319	Pistachio Green, very dark
⫷	367	Pistachio Green, dark
e	368	Pistachio Green, light
/	369	Pistachio Green, very light
■	433	Brown, medium
⌘	435	Brown, very light
3	436	Tan
√	437	Tan, light
6	666	Christmas Red, bright
m	677	Old Gold, very light
S	725	Topaz
H	813	Blue, light
▼	839	Beige Brown, dark
$	840	Beige Brown, medium
//	841	Beige Brown, light
L	842	Beige Brown, very light
✳	912	Emerald Green, light

tips

- If substituting 6-strand embroidery floss for #3 pearl cotton, use six strands for cross stitch. The color numbers would be the same.

- Due to the loose weave in the fabric, it is recommended that a hoop should not be used with this prefinished product.

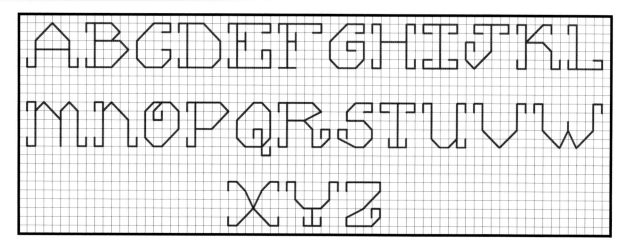

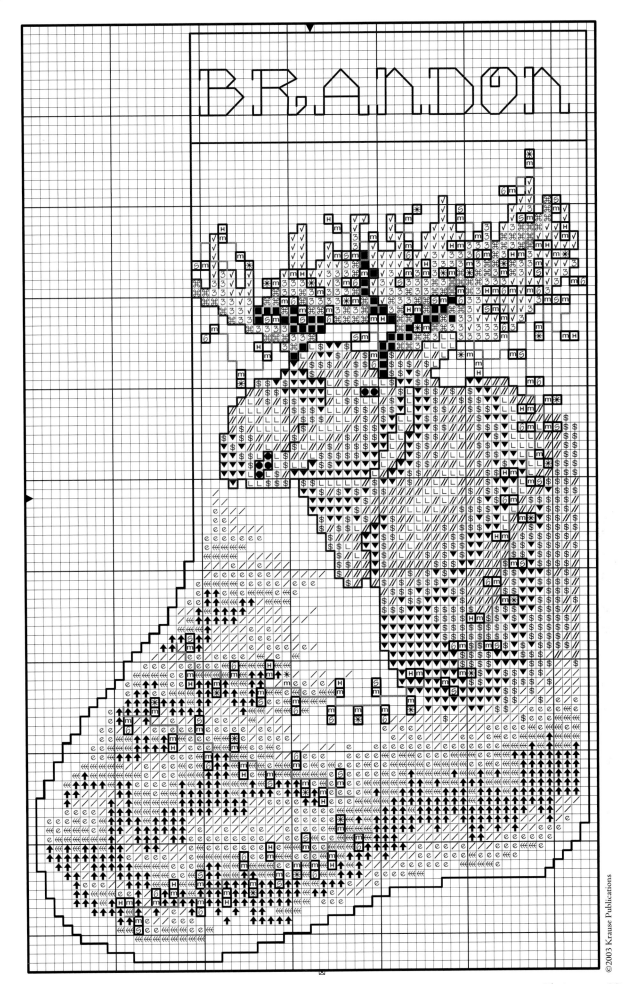

Cross Stitch: 1 strand (#3 pearl cotton)
  or 1 strand (#32 heavy braid)
Backstitch: 1 strand (#32 heavy braid)
  or 2 strands (6-strand embroidery floss)
Stitch Count: 54 wide x 99 high
Approximate Finished Size (7-count):
  7¾" x 14⅛"

Supplies

- Adam Original Prefinished Stocking
  made with Zweigart® 7-count White
  Klostern
- DMC® 11-count White Aida
- DMC® #3 Pearl Cotton
  - 1 skein each #350, #352, #498, #746,
    #783, #798, #799, #910, #912
- Kreinik #32 Heavy Braid™
  - 1 spool each #091, #094, #210, #421,
    #9100, #9194
- Kreinik ¹⁄₁₆" Ribbon (for ornaments)
  - 1 spool each #091, #094, #210, #421,
    #9100, #9194
- DMC® 6-Strand Embroidery Floss
  - 1 skein each #422, #498
- #20 Tapestry Needle (#3 pearl cotton,
  #32 braid, or 6-strand embroidery floss)
- #26 Tapestry Needle (two strands
  embroidery floss)

Ornament Stocking and Ornaments

Design by Mike Vickery
Stocking stitching by Lynda Moss
Ornament stitching by Lois Hiles

Bold, rich colors burst forth on this prefinished stocking—Star Yellow, Star Blue, Gold Dust, Azalea, Sunlight, and Star Green in Kreinik's heavy braid. The 7-count stocking has a zipper in the back, so you can pull out the lining for easier stitching. Coordinate your tree decorations with your stockings. Several of the ornament motifs were made into actual ornaments stitched on 11-count white Aida.

General Instructions

Refer to accompanying alphabet. Count out the letters and spaces in the name before stitching. Measure four rows down from the top to start stitching the name.

Ornament Instructions

Choose ornament motifs from the stocking to make as actual ornaments, as follows:

1. Stitch the ornament motifs on 11-count White Aida, using three strands embroidery floss. Substitute Kreinik ¹/₁₆" Ribbon in place of the Kreinik #32 Heavy Braid™.
2. Attach a piece of white felt to the back of each ornament by hand-sewing around the outer edges of the ornament.
3. Trim the excess felt and Aida to within one square of the stitched area.
4. Apply Fray Check to the edges of the Aida and felt to keep them from unraveling.
5. Make a loop, using one of the metallic threads from the design.
6. Attach the loop to the back of the felt as a hanger.

Other options for finishing: Omit sewing the felt and very lightly glue the felt to the stitched piece around the edges, or omit the felt entirely and use a fabric stiffener. Both of these options would still require trimming the excess Aida to within one square of the stitched area.

Backstitch Instructions

Use DMC® 6-Strand Embroidery Floss on all backstitch in the colors specified below, except the name, which is in Krenik #32 Heavy Braid™.

Around and within ornaments: DMC® 422 Hazelnut Brown, light.

Ribbon and line underneath name: DMC® 498 Christmas Red, dark.

Name: Kreinik 421 Azalea.

tips

- If substituting 6-strand embroidery floss for #3 pearl cotton, use six strands for cross stitch. The color numbers would be the same.

- Due to the loose weave in the fabric, it is recommended that a hoop should not be used with this prefinished product.

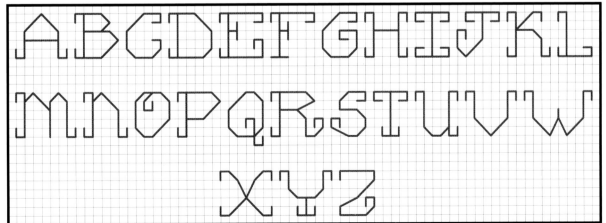

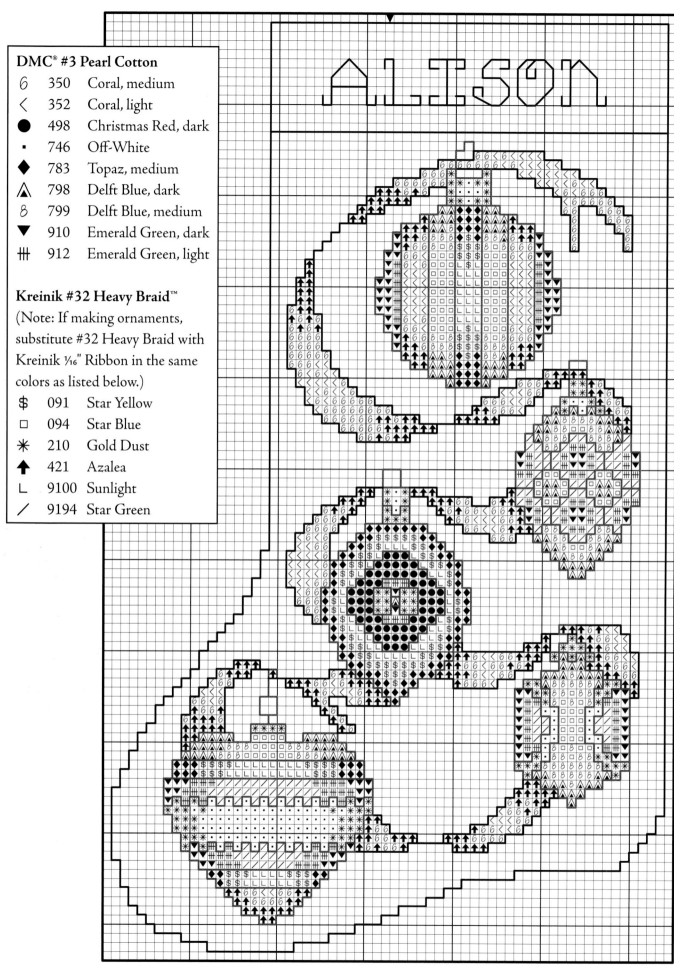

DMC® #3 Pearl Cotton

- 6 350 Coral, medium
- < 352 Coral, light
- ● 498 Christmas Red, dark
- · 746 Off-White
- ◆ 783 Topaz, medium
- ⩕ 798 Delft Blue, dark
- 8 799 Delft Blue, medium
- ▼ 910 Emerald Green, dark
- ⧺ 912 Emerald Green, light

Kreinik #32 Heavy Braid™

(Note: If making ornaments, substitute #32 Heavy Braid with Kreinik ⅟₁₆" Ribbon in the same colors as listed below.)

- \$ 091 Star Yellow
- ☐ 094 Star Blue
- ✳ 210 Gold Dust
- ↑ 421 Azalea
- L 9100 Sunlight
- ╱ 9194 Star Green

For "Ho Ho Ho":
Cross Stitch: 2 strands
Stitch Count: 21 wide x 19 high
Approximate Finished Size (10-count): 2⅛" x 1⅞"

For the decorated tree:
Cross Stitch: 2 strands
Stitch Count: 25 wide x 26 high
Approximate Finished Size (10-count): 2½" square

Supplies
- Adam Original Prefinished Bear Vest made with Zweigart® 10-count Sand Tula®
- DMC® 6-Strand Embroidery Floss
  - 1 skein each #321, #433, #909
- 1 ball DMC® #321 #8 Pearl Cotton
- 1 skein DMC® #5282 6-Strand Metallic Floss
- 26 Mill Hill® Size 6 #16617 Red Glass Beads
- Mill Hill® Large Red Star Glass Treasure #12175
- Mill Hill® Small Red Star Glass Treasure #12172
- #24 Tapestry Needle

Festive Bear Vest

Designs by Phyllis Dobbs
Stitching by Kay Freeman

'Twas the night before Christmas and everyone was ready for Santa ... including this cuddly bear in his festive vest. The Adam Original prefinished vest is embellished with sparkling red star Mill Hill Glass Treasures, gold metallic for the garland, and large red glass beads as tree ornaments. The vest was trimmed with a blanket stitch in Christmas Red along the inner sides of the vest.

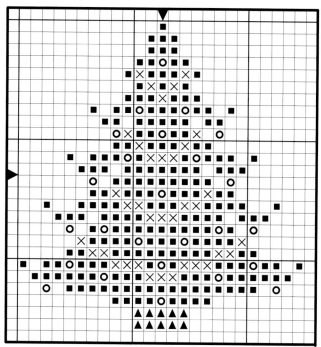

©2003 The DMC® Corporation

©2003 The DMC® Corporation

General Instructions

1. Complete all of the cross stitch first.
2. Attach the beads with DMC® 321 Christmas Red embroidery floss.
3. Do a blanket stitch along the inner sides of vest with DMC® 321 Christmas Red #8 Pearl Cotton. Refer to the stitch diagrams on page 138, if necessary.
4. Attach a large Star Glass Treasure with DMC® 321 Christmas Red embroidery floss about 1" down from the top of the vest and approximately 1½" above "Ho Ho Ho."
5. Attach a small Star Glass Treasure with DMC® 321 Christmas Red embroidery floss at the top of the tree.

	DMC® 6-Strand Embroidery Floss	
▲	433	Brown, medium
■	909	Christmas Green

	DMC® 6-Strand Metallic Floss	
×	5282	Gold

	Mill Hill Size 6 Glass Beads	
○	16617	Red

Cross Stitch: 3 strands (floss)
1 strand (#16 medium braid)
Backstitch: 1 strand (floss)
Bows: 1 strand (⅛" ribbon)
Stitch Count: 130 wide x 79 high (one motif)
Approximate Finished Size (10-count): 13" x 7⅞" (one motif)

Supplies
- Adam Original Prefinished Tartan Plaid Trimmed Tree Skirt made with Zweigart® 10-count White Tula®
- Anchor® 6-Strand Embroidery Floss
  - 1 skein each #244, #401, #1022
  - 2 skeins #19
  - 3 skeins #22
- Kreinik ⅛" Ribbon™
  - 1 spool #008
  - 1 spool #015
- Kreinik #16 Medium Braid™
  - 2 spools #045
  - 3 spools each #101, #210
  - 4 spools each #203, #421
- #22 Tapestry needle

Ornament Tree Skirt

Design by Mike Vickery
Stitching by Lynda Moss

This tree skirt just might receive more attention than the tree. Ornaments adorn the skirt in sparkling Kreinik braids, embellished with green and chartreuse bows constructed of ⅛" ribbon. The prefinished 10-count white Tula tree skirt has a 4" Tartan plaid trim with metallic gold threads running throughout, giving the overall project a unique richness.

General Instructions
Measure down 12 squares from the top center to start the first stitch. Center the design motif. Optional: After stitching on the complete motif in the center, stitch another motif on each side of the center motif, being careful to start each motif in line with the same row where the center motif started.

Bow Instructions
The ● represents where a single bow should be placed. Using ⅛" ribbon to make the bows, alternate with #008 Green and #015 Chartreuse.

tip

Due to the loose weave in the fabric, it is recommended that a hoop should not be used with this prefinished product.

Backstitch Instructions
All backstitch: Anchor® 401 Gray, dark.

Anchor® 6-Strand Embroidery Floss

＄	19	Burgundy, medium
♥	22	Burgundy, very dark
■	244	Grass Green, medium dark
8	1022	Peony, medium light

Kreinik ⅛″ Ribbon™

●	008	Green
●	015	Chartreuse

Kreinik #16 Medium Braid™

▼	045	Confetti Gold
⋘	101	Platinum
6	203	Flame
⊕	210	Gold Dust
⟁	421	Azalea

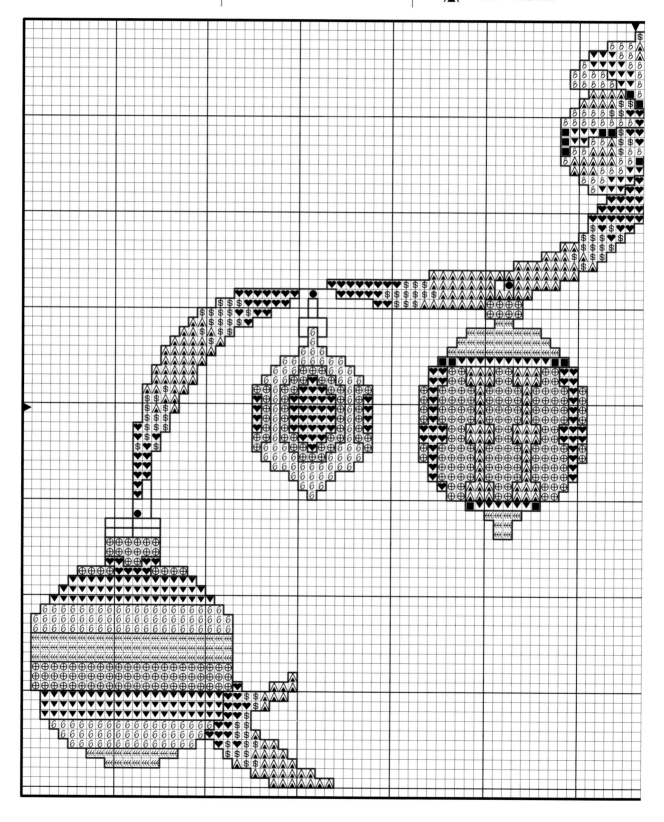

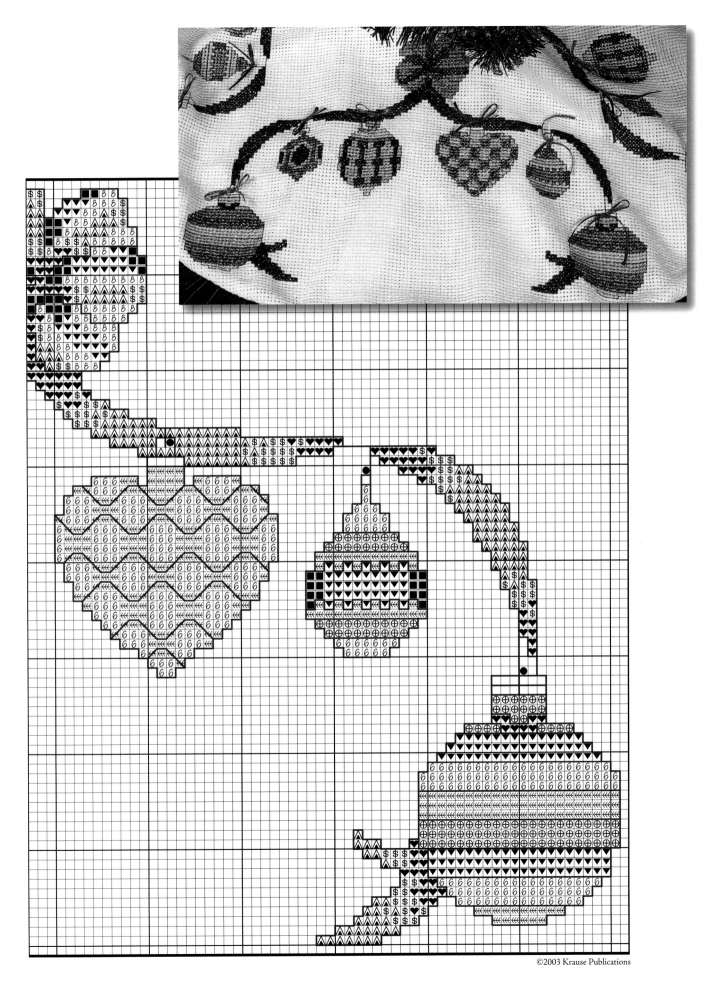

Cross Stitch: 4 strands (floss)
  1 strand (#16 medium braid)
Backstitch: 2 strands (floss)
Stitch Count: 144 wide x 77 high (one complete motif)
Approximate Finished Size (11-count): 13⅛" x 7"

Supplies
- Zweigart® Prefinished 11-count Gold/Cream Metallic Rondo Table Topper
- Anchor® 6-Strand Embroidery Floss
  - 1 skein each #22, #46, #242, #244, #387, #388, #926, #1044
  - 2 skeins #47
- Kreinik #16 Medium Metallic Braid™
  - 7 spools #031
  - 4 spools #032
- #24 Tapestry Needle

Poinsettia Table Topper

Design by Mike Vickery
Stitching by Monica Goodreau

Dazzle your holiday guests with this festive table topper. The gold metallic threads in the fabric coordinate beautifully with the crimson and pearl metallic braids in the poinsettias. This prefinished metallic topper is unique in that you have an option as to which side to stitch on. The project here was stitched on the cream side with gold highlights. The reverse side, originally considered the "right" side until it was discovered that either side was acceptable for stitching, is gold metallic with cream highlights.

General Instructions
1. Find half of the stitch area vertically and do a running stitch with a contrasting color.
2. Center the middle poinsettia.
3. Start stitching on the sixth row from the edge.
4. When one complete motif is stitched, turn the tablecloth to the other side and repeat procedure of stitching as in first motif. Stitching can be on either side of the tablecloth.

	Anchor® 6-Strand Embroidery Floss				Kreinik #16 Medium Braid™	
$	46	Crimson Red		L	031	Crimson
♥	47	Carmine Red		·	032	Pearl
⊕	242	Grass Green, medium light				
▼	244	Grass Green, medium dark				
8	387	Ecru				
+	926	Ecru, very light				
●	1044	Grass Green, ultra dark				

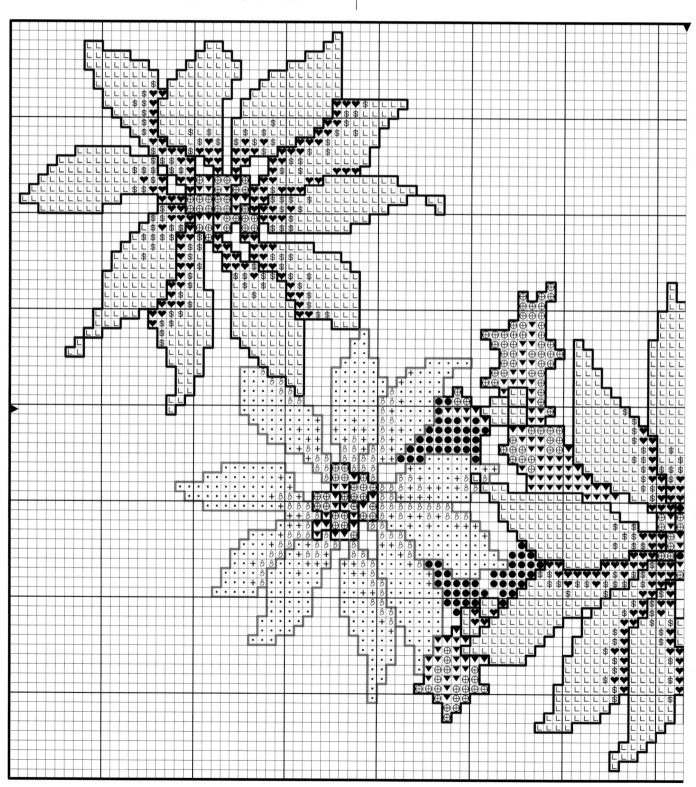

Backstitch Instructions

Red poinsettias, holly berries, and poinsettia centers:
Anchor® 22 Burgundy, very dark.

White poinsettias: Anchor® 388 Ecru, medium.

Holly: Anchor® 1044 Grass Green, ultra dark.

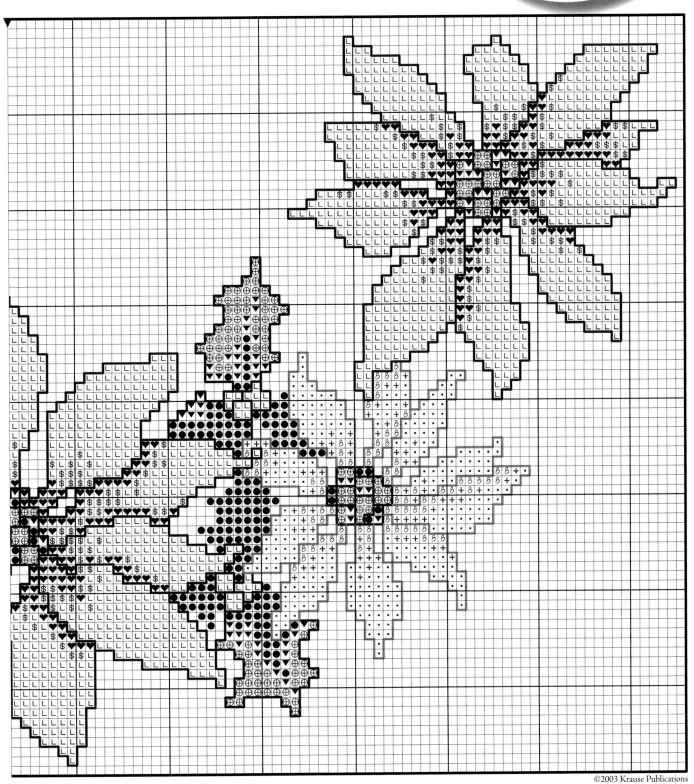

Easy See, Easy Stitch for
Décor and More

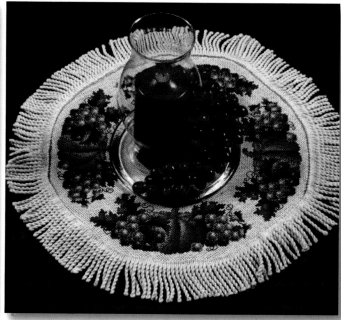

Cross Stitch: 4 strands
Backstitch: 2 strands
Stitch Count: 126 wide x 126 high
Approximate Finished Size (10-count): 12⅝" square

Supplies
- Beautiful Accents™ Prefinished Large Pillow Sham made with Zweigart® 10-count White Tula®
- Anchor® 6-Strand Embroidery Floss
  - 1 skein each #295, #297, #298, #301, #306, #386, #387, #393, #926
  - 2 skeins each #2, #1044
- Anchor® 6-Strand Variegated Floss
  - 2 skeins each #1213, #1215
- 16" Pillow Form
- #22 Tapestry Needle

Daisy Pillow Sham

Design by Mike Vickery
Stitching by Sarah Blalock

These daisies will always be in bloom. White and yellow daisies mingle among variegated green leaves. The Beautiful Accents™ prefinished sham is trimmed with a 2" cluny lace. The design would also look great as a framed picture.

tip

Due to the large size of this chart, it is split into four pieces. Two pieces appear here, and the others appear on the following two pages, along with the keycode and the backstitch instructions.

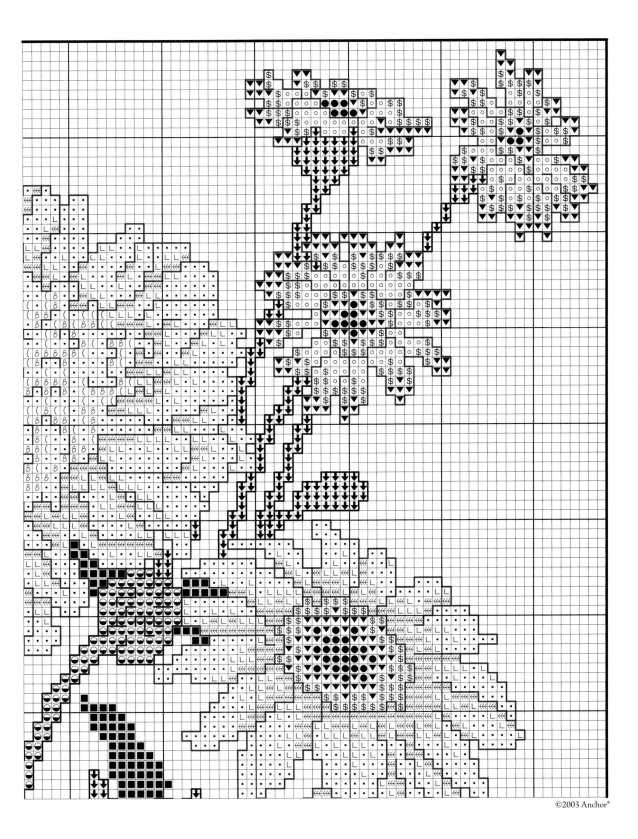

©2003 Anchor®

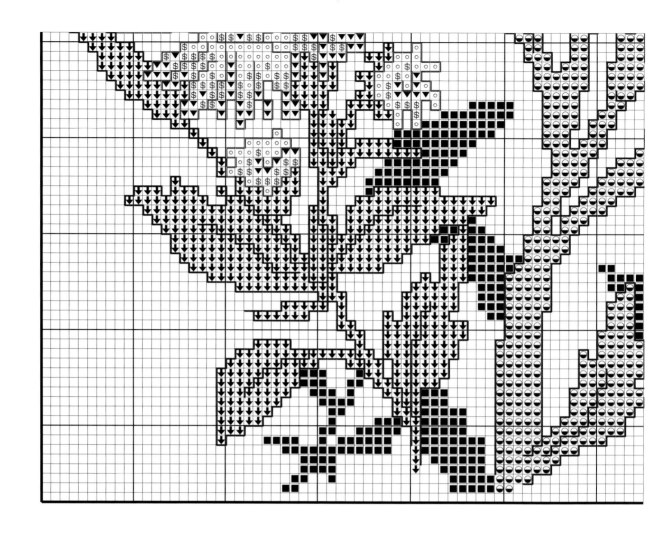

Anchor® 6-Strand Embroidery Floss

·	2	White	●	306	Topaz, medium light
○	295	Jonquil, medium light	(	386	Citrus, very light
$	297	Jonquil, medium	⋘	387	Ecru
▼	298	Jonquil, dark	L	926	Ecru, very light
8	301	Citrus	■	1044	Grass Green, ultra dark

Anchor® 6-Strand Variegated Floss

↓	1213	Christmas Green, light to dark	◒	1215	Moss Green, light to dark

Backstitch Instructions

Yellow daisies and the centers of the white daisies: Anchor® 306 Topaz, medium light.

White daisies: Anchor® 393 Linen, dark.

Leaves and stems: Anchor® 1044 Grass Green, ultra dark.

Cross Stitch: 3 strands
Backstitch: 2 strands
Stitch Count: 54 wide x 26 high
Approximate Finished Size
(10-count): 5⅜" x 2½"

Supplies

- Adam Original Prefinished Checkbook Cover made with Zweigart® 10-count Navy Blue Tula®
- Anchor® 6-Strand Embroidery Floss
  - 1 skein each #1, #48, #49, #50, #259, #264, #266, #267, #292, #293, #380, #387, #874
- #24 Tapestry Needle

Daisy Checkbook Cover

Design by Roberta Madeleine

Jazz up your checkbook holder with cross stitch. Daisies adorn Adams Original's prefinished checkbook cover made with Zweigart® 10-count navy blue Tula®. The checkbook cover is a quick-to-stitch project that is an inexpensive and useful gift item.

Anchor® 6-Strand Embroidery Floss

♡ 1 Snow White	— 259 Loden Green, very light	△ 292 Jonquil, very light
╱ 48 China Rose, very light	★ 264 Avocado, very light	▼ 293 Jonquil, light
⊥ 49 China Rose, light	❘ 266 Avocado, medium light	☐ 387 Ecru
▲ 50 China Rose, medium	● 267 Avocado, medium	■ 874 Saffron, medium

Backstitch Instructions

All backstitch:
Anchor® 380 Fudge.

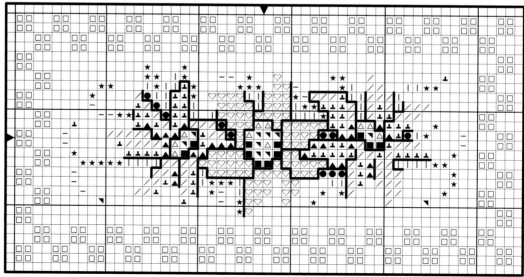

Four Seasons
Candle Doilies

Designs by Pamela Kellogg
Stitching by Kim Dennett

Be innovative! These beautiful candle doilies are actually tabletop tree skirts.
Using the tree skirts as doilies makes it possible to enjoy them year-round.
Savor each season with coordinating candles and the seasonal doilies. These
little beauties make great gift items, too.

Spring Candle Doily

Cross Stitch: 4 strands
Backstitch: 2 strands
French Knots: 2 strands wrapped twice
Stitch Count: 68 wide x 69 high
(one complete motif)
Approximate Finished Size (10-count): 6⅞" circle

Supplies

- Zweigart® Prefinished 10-count Tula™ Cream Doily (Tabletop Tree Skirt)
- DMC® 6-Strand Embroidery Floss
  - 1 skein each White, #153, #154, #740, #741, #742, #743, #772, #895, #3345, #3346, #3347, #3348, #3834, #3835, #3836
  - 2 skeins each #744, #745, #3823
- #22 Tapestry Needle

General Instructions

Careful counting is essential for proper centering of the four motifs.

1. Find the center of the doily.
2. Fold the doily in half again and one motif should fit within each quarter section of the doily.
3. Stitch one complete motif.
4. Leave one blank row between each motif. The chart shows a partial repeat of the design for ease in starting the next motif.

DMC® 6-Strand Embroidery Floss

O	White	White	▲	895	Hunter Green, very dark
◖	153	Light Lavender	m	3345	Hunter Green, dark
■	154	Plum, dark	➜	3346	Hunter Green
◩	740	Tangerine	//	3347	Yellow Green, medium
2	741	Tangerine, medium	∩	3348	Yellow Green, light
✕	742	Tangerine, light	✖	3823	Yellow, very pale
♡	743	Yellow, medium	3	3834	Grape, dark
★	744	Yellow, pale	♥	3835	Grape, medium
Z	745	Yellow, light pale	⬎	3836	Grape, light
4	772	Yellow Green, very light			

Backstitch Instructions

Pansies: DMC® 154 Plum, dark.

Daffodils: DMC® 742 Tangerine, light.

Leaves and curlicues: DMC® 895 Hunter Green, very dark.

Daffodil centers: DMC® 3823 Yellow, very pale.

French Knots

- Daffodil centers: DMC® 3823 Yellow, very pale.

Due to the loose weave in the fabric, it is recommended that a hoop should not be used with this prefinished product.

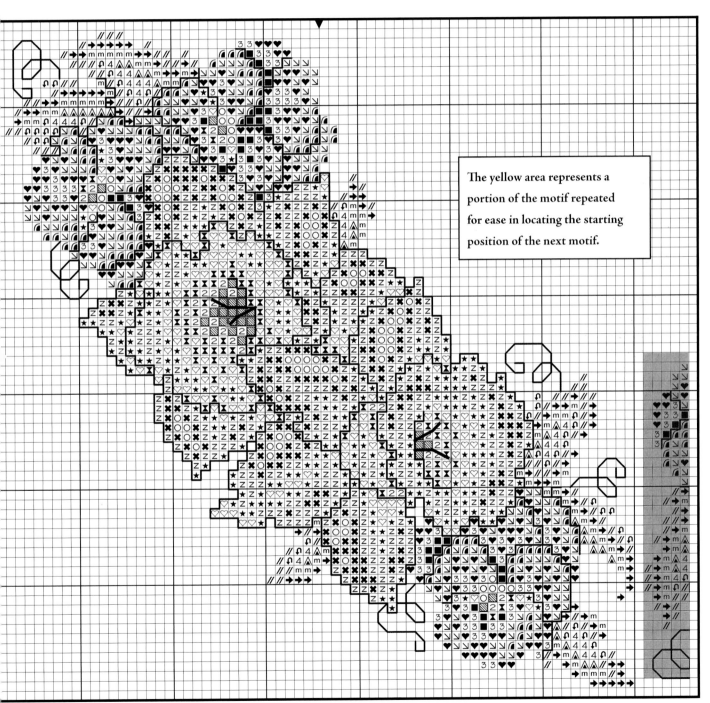

The yellow area represents a portion of the motif repeated for ease in locating the starting position of the next motif.

Summer Candle Doily

Cross Stitch: 4 strands
Backstitch: 2 strands
Stitch Count: 68 wide x 68 high (one complete motif)
Approximate Finished Size (10-count): 6⅞" circle

Supplies

- Zweigart® Prefinished 10-count Tula™ Cream Doily (Tabletop Tree Skirt)
- DMC® 6-Strand Embroidery Floss
  - 1 skein each #433, #434, #772, #780, #782, #801, #814, #815, #816, #895, #898, #938, #3345, #3346, #3347, #3348
  - 2 skeins each #304, #321, #498, #666, #783, #3078, #3705, #3801, #3820, #3821, #3822, #3823
- #22 Tapestry Needle

General Instructions

Careful counting is essential for proper centering of the four motifs.
1. Find the center of the doily.
2. Fold the doily in half again and one motif should fit within each quarter section of the doily.
3. Stitch one complete motif.
4. Leave one blank row between each motif. The chart shows a partial repeat of the design for ease in starting the next motif.

DMC® 6-Strand Embroidery Floss

☆ 304	Christmas Red, medium	m 801 Coffee Brown, dark
◗ 321	Christmas Red	▨ 815 Garnet, medium
⊟ 433	Brown, medium	♡ 816 Garnet
⊘ 434	Brown, light	◖ 895 Hunter Green, very dark
✕ 498	Christmas Red, dark	☻ 898 Coffee Brown, very dark
3 666	Christmas Red, bright	○ 3078 Golden Yellow, very light
♫ 772	Yellow Green, very light	// 3345 Hunter Green, dark
■ 782	Topaz, dark	➔ 3346 Hunter Green
2 783	Topaz, medium	

¢ 3347	Yellow Green, medium
▼ 3348	Yellow Green, light
4 3705	Melon, dark
✪ 3801	Christmas Red, light
♥ 3820	Straw, dark
Z 3821	Straw
✖ 3822	Straw, light
★ 3823	Yellow, very pale

Backstitch Instructions

Yellow roses: DMC® 780 Topaz, ultra very dark.

Poppies: DMC® 814 Garnet, dark.

Leaves and curlicues: DMC® 895 Hunter Green, very dark.

Poppy centers: DMC® 938 Coffee Brown, ultra dark.

Due to the loose weave in the fabric, it is recommended that a hoop should not be used with this prefinished product.

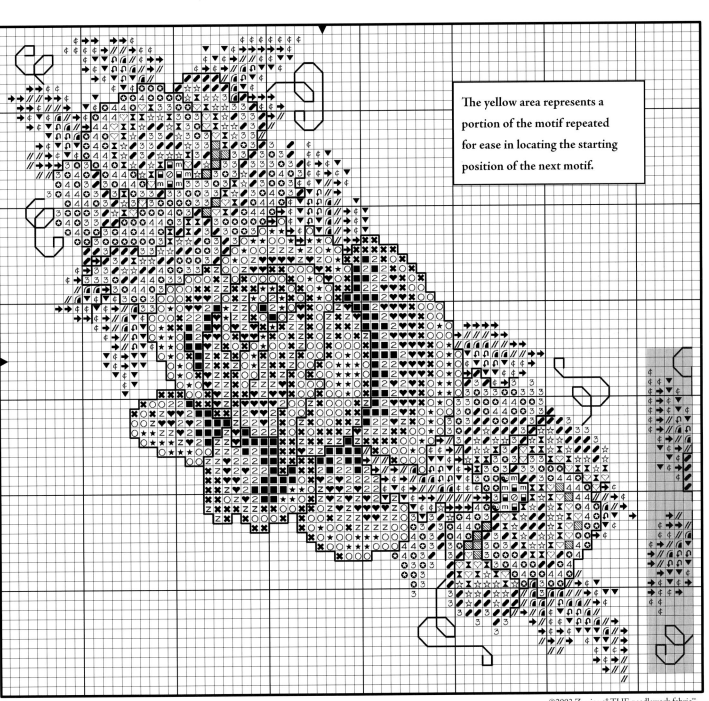

The yellow area represents a portion of the motif repeated for ease in locating the starting position of the next motif.

Autumn Candle Doily

Cross Stitch: 4 strands
Backstitch: 2 strands
Stitch Count: 66 wide x 65 high (one complete motif)
Approximate Finished Size (10-count): 6⅝" circle

Supplies

- Zweigart® Prefinished 10-count Tula™ Cream Doily (Tabletop Tree Skirt)
- DMC® 6-Strand Embroidery Floss
  - 1 skein each White, #153, #154, #400, #433, #434, #435, #436, #437, #745, #772, #801, #895, #898, #3345, #3346, #3347, #3348, #3853, #3854, #3855
  - 2 skeins each #301, #3834, #3835, #3836
- #22 Tapestry Needle

General Instructions

Careful counting is essential to proper centering of four motifs.
1. Find the center of the doily.
2. Fold the doily in half again and one motif should fit within each quarter section of the doily.
3. Stitch one complete motif.
4. Leave **four** blank rows between each motif. (Note: The other three seasonal doilies have only one blank row between each motif.) Chart shows a partial repeat of design for ease in starting the next motif.

DMC® 6-Strand Embroidery Floss

O	White	White	★	745	Yellow, light pale	⬡	3835	Grape, medium
→	153	Lavender, light	☆	772	Yellow Green, very light	//	3836	Grape, light
☍	154	Plum, dark	∩	801	Coffee Brown, dark	Z	3853	Autumn Gold, dark
◆	301	Mahogany, medium	▨	895	Hunter Green, very dark	⬮	3854	Autumn Gold, medium
▫	400	Mahogany, dark	■	898	Coffee Brown, very dark	::	3855	Autumn Gold, light
✖	433	Brown, medium	△	3345	Hunter Green, dark			
2	434	Brown, light	◖	3346	Hunter Green			
✕	435	Brown, very light	3	3347	Yellow Green, medium			
♡	436	Tan	♥	3348	Yellow Green, light			
m	437	Tan, light	4	3834	Grape, dark			

Blend One Strand of Each Color

=	301	Mahogany, medium <u>and</u>
	400	Mahogany, dark

Backstitch Instructions

Grapes: DMC® 154 Plum, dark.

Pumpkin: DMC® 400 Mahogany, dark.

Pumpkin stem: DMC® 433 Brown, medium.

Grape leaves and curlicues: DMC® 895 Hunter Green, very dark.

Oak leaves: DMC® 898 Coffee Brown, very dark.

Due to the loose weave in the fabric, it is recommended that a hoop should not be used with this prefinished product.

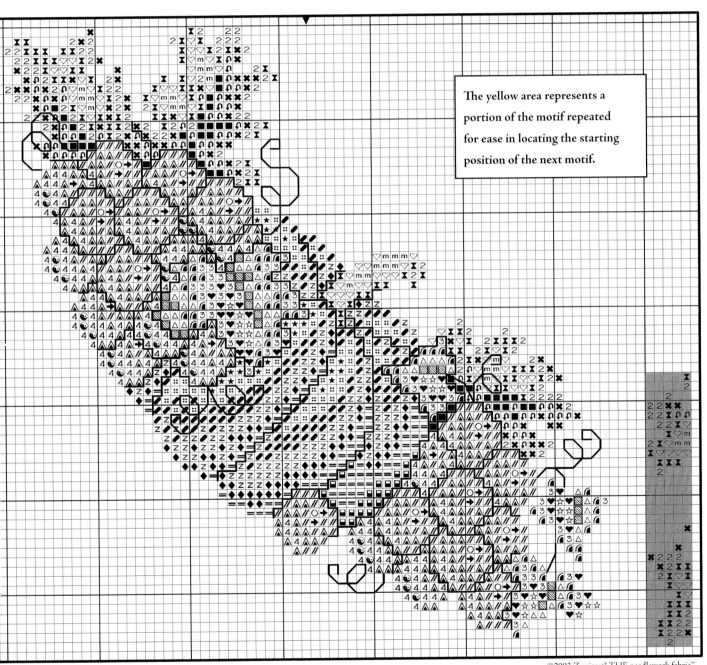

The yellow area represents a portion of the motif repeated for ease in locating the starting position of the next motif.

Cross Stitch: 4 strands
Backstitch: 2 strands
Stitch Count: 65 wide x 68 high
(one complete motif)
Approximate Finished Size (10-count):
6⅝" x 6⅞"

Supplies

- Zweigart® prefinished 10-count Tula™ Cream Doily (tabletop tree skirt)
- DMC® 6-Strand Embroidery Floss
  - 1 skein each White, #304, #321, #433, #434, #435, #436, #437, #498, #666, #738, #772, #801, #814, #816, #895, #898, #938, #3705, #3801
  - 2 skeins each #3345, #3346, #3348
  - 3 skeins #3347
- #22 Tapestry Needle

General Instructions

Careful counting is essential for proper centering of the four motifs.

1. Find the center of the doily.
2. Fold the doily in half again and one motif should fit within each quarter section of the doily.
3. Stitch one complete motif.
4. Leave one blank row between each motif. The chart shows a partial repeat of the design for ease in starting the next motif.

DMC® 6-Strand Embroidery Floss

◒	White	White	¢	666	Christmas Red, bright	■	938	Coffee Brown, ultra dark
↘	304	Christmas Red, medium	☆	738	Tan, very light	♡	3345	Hunter Green, dark
◢	321	Christmas Red	3	772	Yellow Green, very light	◪	3346	Hunter Green
♥	433	Brown, medium	2	801	Coffee Brown, dark	Z	3347	Yellow Green, medium
m	434	Brown, light	▄	814	Garnet, dark	→	3348	Yellow Green, light
✖	435	Brown, very light	4	816	Garnet	I	3705	Melon, dark
∩	436	Tan	▧	895	Hunter Green, very dark	★	3801	Christmas Red, light
✖	437	Tan, light	△	898	Coffee Brown, very dark			
▲	498	Christmas Red, dark						

Backstitch Instructions

Berries: DMC® 814 Garnet, dark.

Leaves: DMC® 895 Hunter Green, very dark.

All other backstitch: DMC® 938 Coffee Brown, ultra dark.

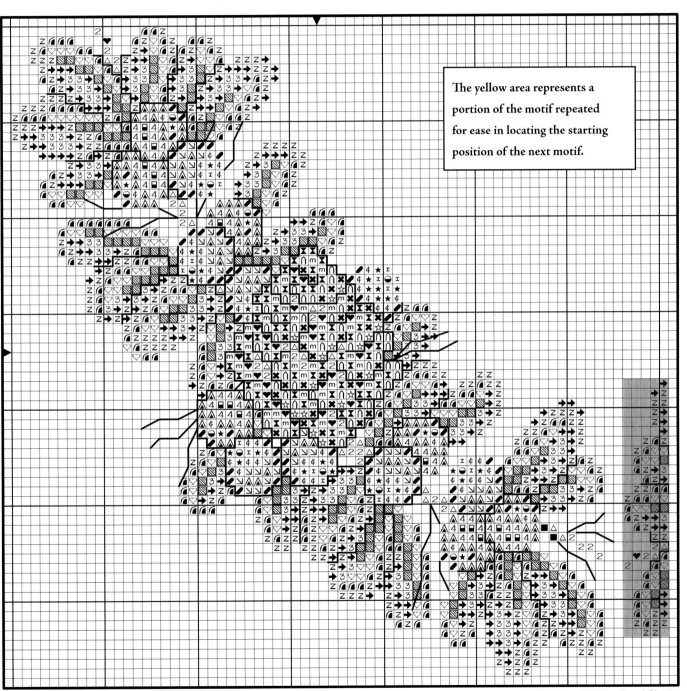

The yellow area represents a portion of the motif repeated for ease in locating the starting position of the next motif.

Cross Stitch: 4 strands
  (or 3 strands)
Backstitch: 2 strands
French Knots: 2 strands
  wrapped twice
Stitch Count: 90 wide x 70 high
Approximate Finished Size
  (11-count): 8⅛" x 6⅓"

Supplies
- DMC® 11-count White Aida
- DMC® 6-Strand Embroidery
  Floss
  - 1 skein each White, #310,
    #317, #318, #321, #413,
    #414, #415, #666, #762,
    #772, #776, #818, #819,
    #895, #3345, #3346, #3347,
    #3348, #3705, #3706, #3708,
    #3799, #3801
- #24 or #26 Tapestry Needle
- 7" x 9" Frame

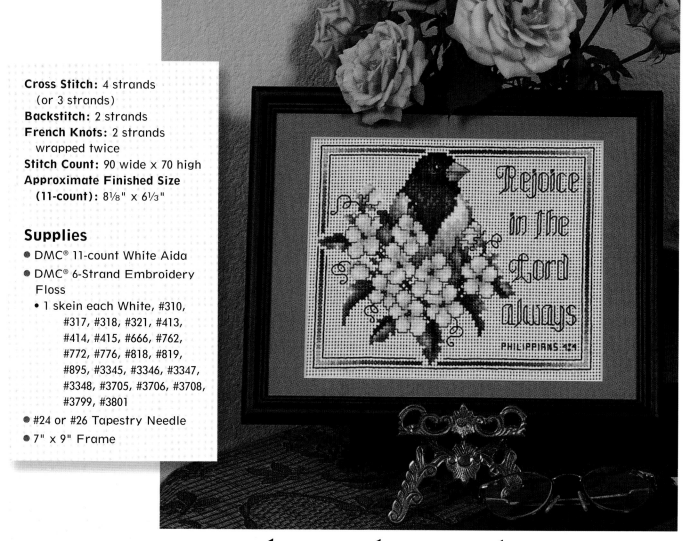

Rejoice in the Lord Framed Piece

Design by Pamela Kellogg
Stitching by Lois Hiles

The colorful Grosbeak among the delicate pink blossoms brings an inspiring message to guide us in our daily lives. Stitched on 11-count Aida, this project is completed in a short time. You may want to stitch one for a gift and keep one for yourself.

DMC® 6-Strand Embroidery Floss

O	White	White	♡	666	Christmas Red, bright	✎	3346	Hunter Green
■	310	Black	3	762	Pearl Gray, very light	//	3347	Yellow Green, medium
Z	317	Pewter Gray	↘	772	Yellow Green, very light	⋀	3348	Yellow Green, light
2	318	Steel Gray, light	✕	776	Pink, medium	⋂	3705	Melon, dark
▧	321	Christmas Red	☆	818	Baby Pink	⌐	3706	Melon, medium
♥	413	Pewter Gray, dark	♠	819	Baby Pink, light	m	3708	Melon, light
✪	414	Steel Gray, dark	☻	895	Hunter Green, very dark	4	3799	Pewter Gray, very dark
✖	415	Pearl Gray	¢	3345	Hunter Green, dark	★	3801	Christmas Red, light

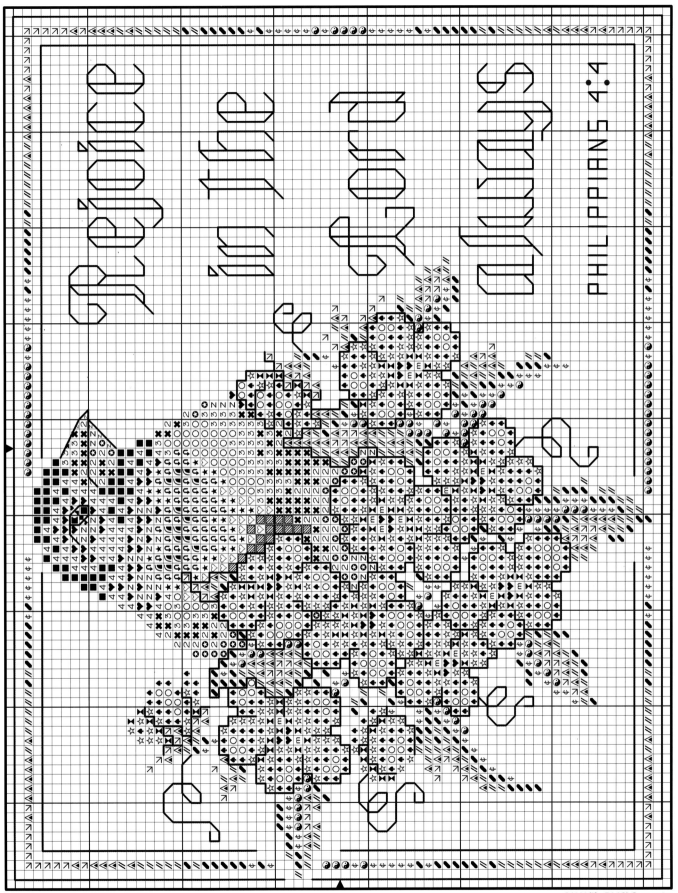

rejoice in the Lord always

PHILIPPIANS 4:4

Backstitch Instructions

Bird's eye: DMC® 310 Black.
Flowers and the bird's beak: DMC® 317 Pewter Gray.
Border, leaves, and curlicues: DMC® 895 Hunter Green, very dark.
Lettering: DMC® 3799, Pewter Gray, very dark.

French Knots

o Bird's eye: DMC® White.
● Lettering: DMC® 3799 Pewter Gray, very dark.

This inspirational design would also look lovely finished as a pillow.

Cross Stitch: 3 strands
Backstitch: 1 strand

Supplies

- Zweigart® Prefinished Delft Blue 10-count Oktav Table Topper or Zweigart® Prefinished White 10-count Oktav Table Topper
- Anchor® 6-Strand Embroidery Floss
  - 6 skeins #131 (white topper) or #1 (blue topper)
- #24 Tapestry Needle

Lace Border Table Toppers

These lace-themed toppers will fool even the most discriminating guests, as the lace border gives the prefinished table toppers a look of true lace elegance. This design provides options that result in two totally different appearances. To achieve the look of real lace, the stitcher used white floss on a delft blue Oktav table topper. For the white table topper, a medium cobalt blue floss was used.

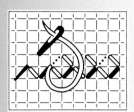

tip

If you work the cross stitch garland and outer edges first, the net pattern will fit in almost without counting. Work the net pattern in rows. Work every other stitch in the first row across and fill in the spaces on the return journey, as shown. In this way, the pattern looks identical on the right and wrong sides of the fabric.

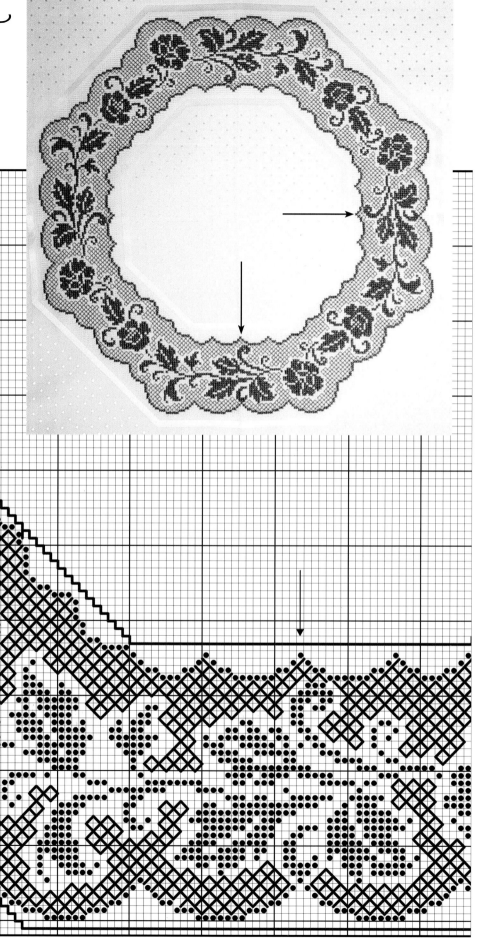

General Instructions

Black borders are not to be stitched. They represent guidelines for the stitching area within the table topper. Study the chart and the photograph closely for placement. The area between the two long arrows represents one-quarter of the design that is stitched four times.

Anchor® 6-Strand Embroidery Floss

(For stitching on White Table Topper)
● 131   Cobalt Blue, medium

(For stitching on Delft Blue Table Topper)
● 1   White

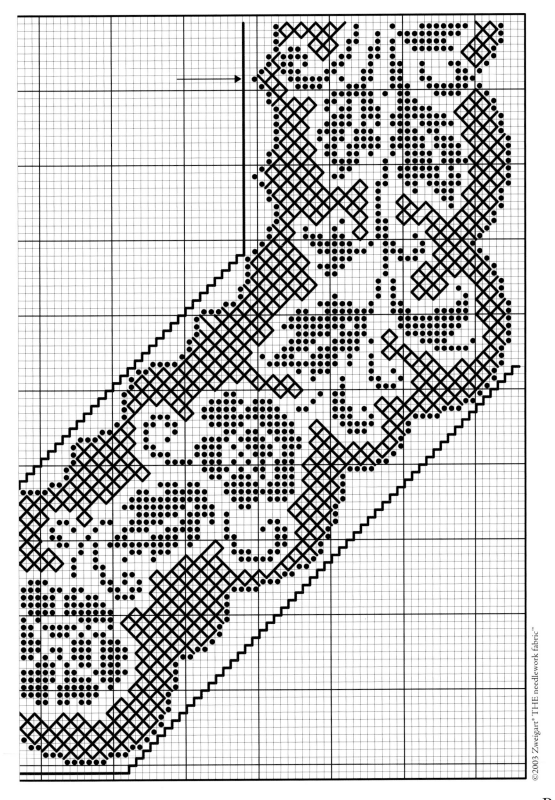

©2003 Zweigart® THE needlework fabric™

Rhode Island Red Rooster and Buff Orpington Hen Pillow Shams and Framed Pieces

Designs by Mike Vickery
Stitching of framed pieces by Lois Hiles
Stitching of hen pillow sham by Donna Barrett

Add some colorful rural charm to your décor with this rooster and hen set. The fowls are featured on Adam Original's prefinished 10-count pillow shams, which are trimmed with hunter green ruffles. Then, the rooster and hen take the spotlight again as framed pieces for the kitchen. Yet another idea for this pair is to omit the lettering and border and stitch one on a Largo 10-count table topper.

tip

Due to the loose weave in the fabric, it is recommended that a hoop should not be used with this prefinished pillow sham.

Rhode Island Red Rooster

Cross Stitch: 3 strands (pillow sham)
2 strands (framed piece)
Backstitch: 2 strands (pillow sham)
1 strand (#3799) (framed piece)
3 strands (#319) (framed piece)
Stitch Count: 140 wide x 140 high (both)
Approximate Finished Sizes:
14" square (10-count pillow sham)
12¾" square (11-count framed piece)

Supplies (pillow sham)
- Adam Original Prefinished Pillow Sham with Hunter Green Ruffle made with Zweigart® 10-count Beige Tula
- DMC® 6-Strand Embroidery Floss
  - 1 skein each #317, #318, #319, #349, #351, #352, #725, #727, #783, #918, #920, #3799, #3825
  - 2 skeins #922
- #24 or #26 Tapestry Needle

Supplies (framed piece)
- 11-count DMC® White Aida
- DMC® 6-Strand Embroidery Floss
  - 1 skein each color listed for the pillow sham
- #26 Tapestry Needle
- 14" Square Frame

Cross Stitch: 4 strands (pillow sham)
2 strands (framed piece)
Backstitch: 1 strand (#3799) (both)
3 strands (#319) (both)
Stitch Count: 140 wide x 140 high (both)
Approximate Finished Sizes:
14" square (10-count pillow sham)
12¾" square (11-count framed piece)

Supplies (pillow sham)
- Adam Original Prefinished Pillow Sham with Hunter Green Ruffle made with Zweigart® 10-count Beige Tula
- DMC® 6-Strand Embroidery Floss
  - 1 skein each #319, #349, #351, #352, #725, #727, #783, #3799, #3852
  - 2 skeins each #3820, #3821, #3822
- #24 or #26 Tapestry Needle

Supplies (framed piece)
- 11-count DMC® White Aida
- DMC® 6-Strand Embroidery Floss
  - 1 skein each color listed for the pillow sham
- #26 Tapestry Needle
- 13" Square or Custom Frame

Buff Orpington Hen

DMC® 6-Strand Embroidery Floss

✖	317	Pewter Gray	⟩	352	Coral, light	$	920	Copper, medium
3	318	Steel Gray, light	#	725	Topaz	=	922	Copper, light
■	319	Pistachio Green, very dark	/	727	Topaz, very light	●	3799	Pewter Gray, very dark
♥	349	Coral, dark	↑	783	Topaz, medium			
6	351	Coral	▲	918	Red Copper, dark	√	3825	Pumpkin, pale

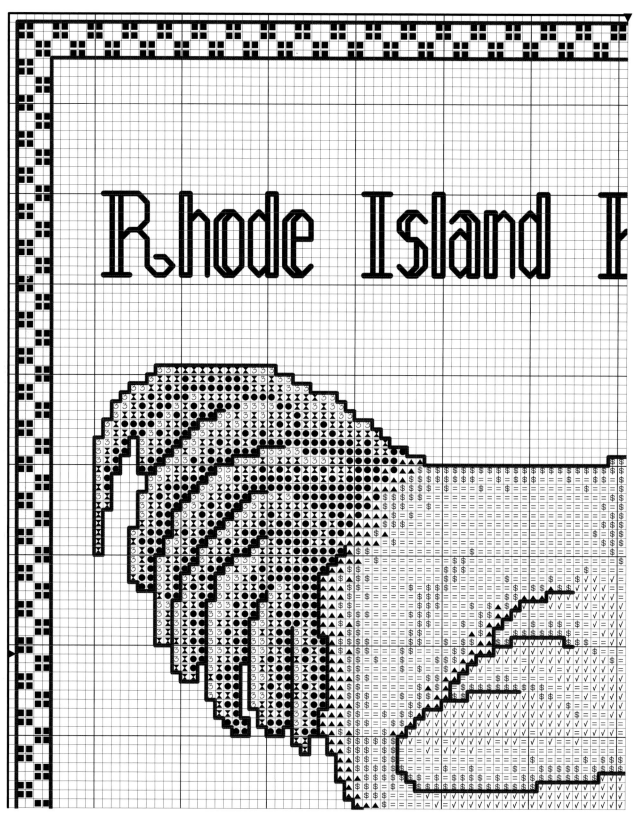

Backstitch Instructions

Lettering: DMC® 319 Pistachio Green, very dark.
All other backstitch: DMC® 3799 Pewter Gray,
very dark.

Due to the size of the stitching chart, it is split into four pieces. Two parts appear here with the keycode and the remaining two parts are on the following pages.

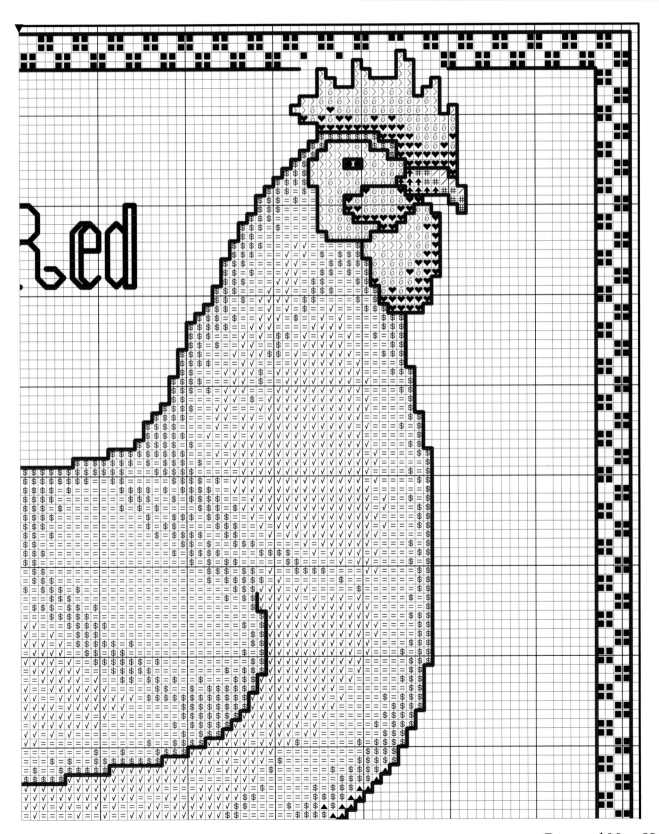

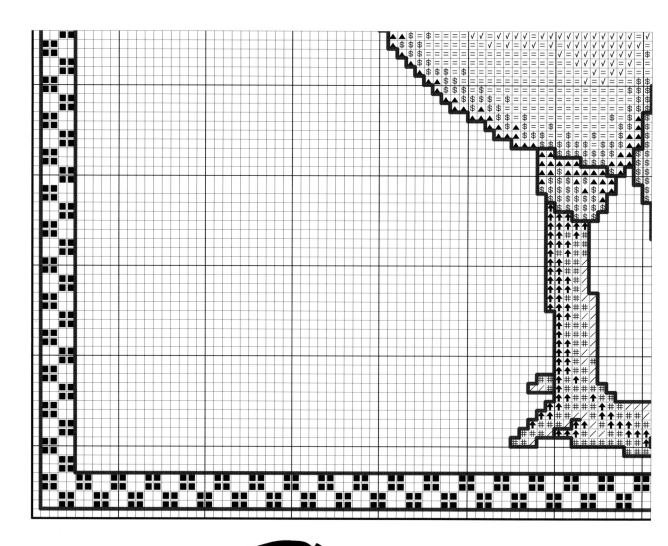

DMC® 6-Strand Embroidery Floss*

✘	317	Pewter Gray
3	318	Steel Gray, light
■	319	Pistachio Green, very dark
♥	349	Coral, dark
6	351	Coral
⟩	352	Coral, light
#	725	Topaz
/	727	Topaz, very light
↑	783	Topaz, medium
▲	918	Red Copper, dark
$	920	Copper, medium
=	922	Copper, light
●	3799	Pewter Gray, very dark
✓	3825	Pumpkin, pale

*Keycode repeated here for your convenience.

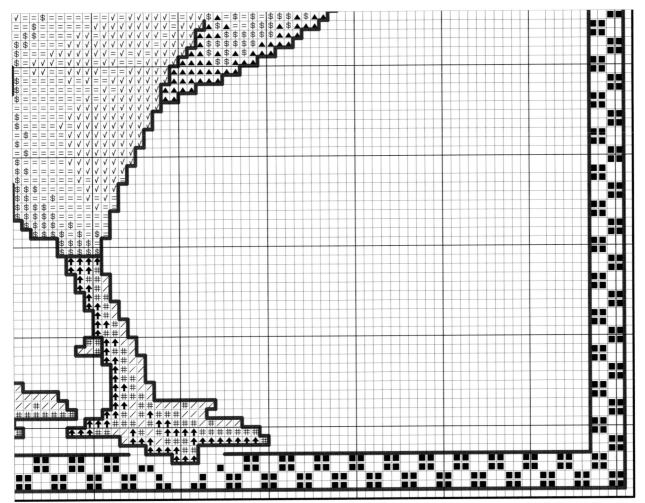

DMC® 6-Strand Embroidery Floss

■	319	Pistachio Green, very dark	
♥	349	Coral, dark	
6	351	Coral	
>	352	Coral, light	
#	725	Topaz	
/	727	Topaz, very light	

↑	783	Topaz, medium	
●	3799	Pewter Gray, very dark	
⋘	3820	Straw, dark	
+	3821	Straw	
·	3822	Straw, light	
⊕	3852	Straw, very dark	

Backstitch Instructions

Lettering: DMC® 319 Pistachio Green, very dark.
All other backstitch: DMC® 3799 Pewter Gray, very dark.

Due to the size of the stitching chart, it is split into four pieces. Two parts appear here with the keycode, and the remaining two parts are on the following pages.

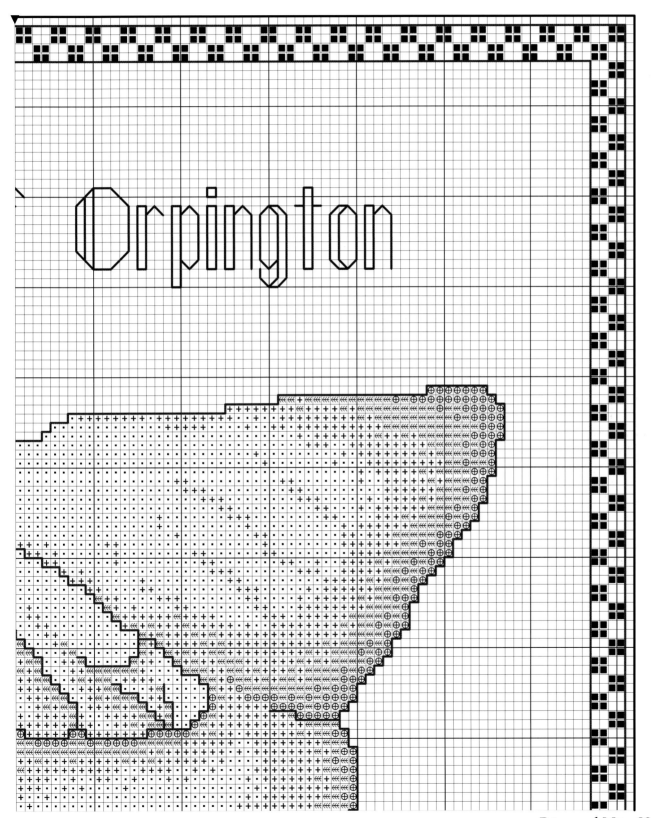

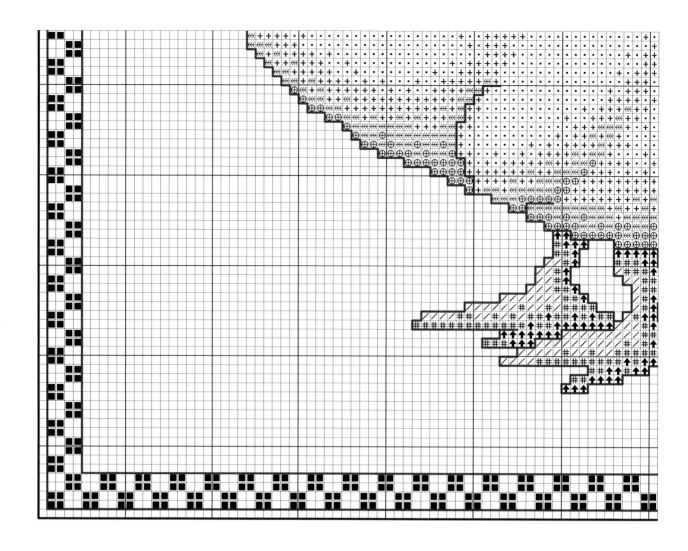

DMC® 6-Strand Embroidery Floss*

■	319	Pistachio Green, very dark
♥	349	Coral, dark
6	351	Coral
⟩	352	Coral, light
#	725	Topaz
/	727	Topaz, very light
↑	783	Topaz, medium
●	3799	Pewter Gray, very dark
⫷	3820	Straw, dark
+	3821	Straw
·	3822	Straw, light
⊕	3852	Straw, very dark

*Keycode repeated here for your convenience.

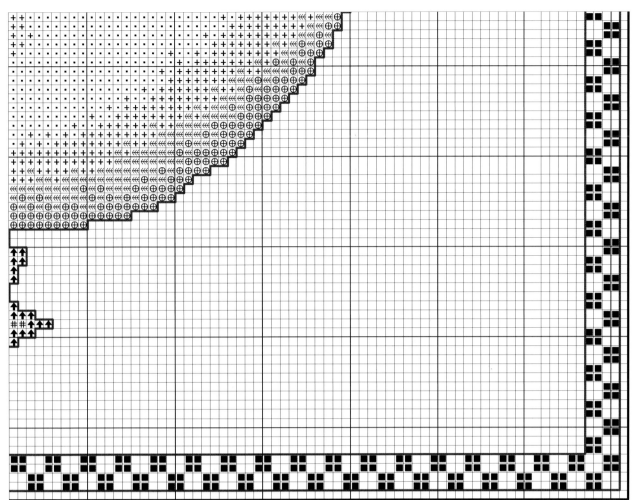

Cross Stitch: 4 strands
Backstitch: 2 strands
Stitch Count: 88 wide x 22 high
Approximate Finished Size (8-count): 11" x 2¾"

Supplies

- Zweigart® 8-count White Cottage Huck Towel with Pistachio Trim #016
- DMC® 6-Strand Embroidery Floss
  - 1 skein each #433, #434, #435, #436, #561, #562, #563, #564, #796, #797, #798, #799, #800, #801, #809, #820, #955, #964, #991, #992, #993, #3814
- #24 Tapestry Needle

Grape Cottage Huck Towel

Design by Pamela Kellogg
Stitching by Kim Dennett

Grapes have increasingly gained popularity in decorative items—especially blue grapes. The checkered border is a nice complement to the grape theme on the easy-to-stitch 8-count cottage huck towel.

DMC® 6-Strand Embroidery Floss

//	433	Brown, medium
➜	434	Brown, light
☆	435	Brown, very light
◓	436	Tan
★	561	Jade, very dark
4	562	Jade, medium
⬛	563	Jade, light
⊘	564	Jade, very light
2	796	Royal Blue, dark
◢	797	Royal Blue
$	798	Delft Blue, dark
♥	799	Deft Blue, medium
✖	800	Delft Blue, pale
❽	801	Coffee Brown, dark
∩	809	Delft Blue
⬛	820	Royal Blue, very dark
⧺	955	Nile Green, light
⊥	964	Sea Green, light
▨	991	Aquamarine, dark
◖	992	Aquamarine, medium
♡	993	Aquamarine, light
3	3814	Aquamarine

Backstitch Instructions

Leaves: DMC® 561 Jade, very dark.
Grapes: DMC® 820 Royal Blue, very dark.
All other backstitch: DMC® 801 Coffee Brown, dark.

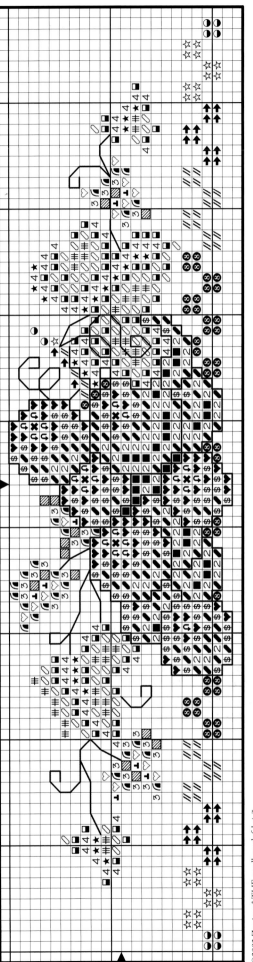

Cross Stitch: 4 strands
Backstitch: 2 strands
French Knots: 2 strands wrapped twice
Stitch Count: 88 wide x 22 high
Approximate Finished Size (8-count): 11" x 2¾"

Supplies

- Zweigart® 8-count White Cottage Huck Towel with Pistachio Trim #016
- DMC® 6-Strand Embroidery Floss
  - 1 skein each #433, #434, #435, #436, #561, #562, #563, #564, #782, #783, #801, #898, #955, #964, #991, #992, #993, #3078, #3685, #3687, #3688, #3689, #3803, #3814, #3820, #3821, #3822, #3823
  - #24 Tapestry Needle

Gooseberry Cottage Huck Towel

Design by Pamela Kellogg
Stitching by Kim Dennett

Red berries accompany gooseberries on a white cottage huck towel that is trimmed with a pistachio floral. This design also has a checkered border to complement the fruit on the quick-to-stitch 8-count towel.

DMC® 6-Strand Embroidery Floss

➜	433	Brown, medium
?	434	Brown, light
❽	435	Brown, very light
⬟	436	Tan
◩	561	Jade, very dark
⋒	562	Jade, medium
◖	563	Jade, light
↘	564	Jade, very light
▬	783	Topaz, medium
$	801	Coffee Brown, dark
▼	898	Coffee Brown, very dark
✚	955	Nile Green, light
♠	964	Sea Green, light
★	991	Aquamarine, dark
✖	992	Aquamarine, medium
//	993	Aquamarine, light
⌐	3078	Golden Yellow, very light
■	3685	Mauve, dark
♥	3687	Mauve
m	3688	Mauve, medium
⬗	3689	Mauve, light
3	3803	Mauve, medium dark
4	3814	Aquamarine
☆	3820	Straw, dark
✪	3821	Straw
♡	3822	Straw, light
Z	3823	Yellow, very pale

Backstitch Instructions

Gooseberries: DMC® 782 Topaz, dark.
Stems and curlicues: DMC® 898 Coffee Brown, very dark.
Red berries: DMC® 3685 Mauve, dark.

French Knot Instructions

● Berry accents: DMC® 898 Coffee Brown, very dark.

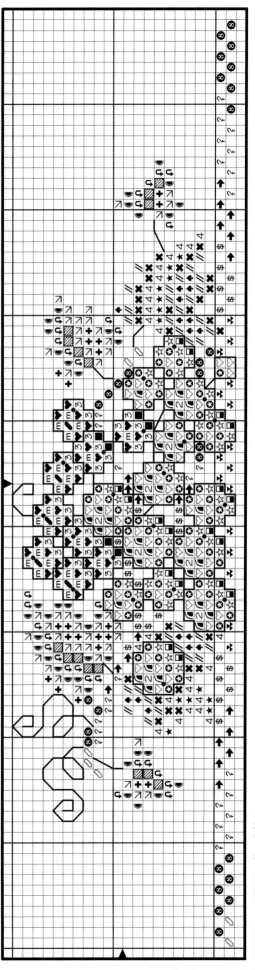

©2003 Zweigart® THE needlework fabric™

Cross Stitch: 4 strands
Backstitch: 2 strands
Stitch Count: 89 wide x 22 high
Approximate Finished Size (8-count): 11" x 2¾"

Supplies

- Zweigart® 8-count White Cottage Huck Towel with Pink Trim #014
- DMC® 6-Strand Embroidery Floss
  - 1 skein each #433, #434, #435, #436, #561, #562, #563, #564, #801, #898, #955, #964, #991, #992, #993, #3685, #3687, #3688, #3689, #3803, #3814
- #24 Tapestry Needle

Cherry Cottage Huck Towel

Design by Pamela Kellogg
Stitching by Kim Dennett

The mauve and burgundy-toned cherries go beautifully with the pink floral trim on this white cottage huck towel. The third of the fruit towel set also shares the spotlight with a checkered border, accentuating the brown palette of the cherry stems.

DMC® 6-Strand Embroidery Floss

♫	433	Brown, medium
◖	434	Brown, light
2	435	Brown, very light
☞	436	Tan
✕	561	Jade, very dark
⬯	562	Jade, medium
★	563	Jade, light
♡	564	Jade, very light
⬓	801	Coffee Brown, dark
➔	898	Coffee Brown, very dark
✖	955	Nile Green, light
◤	964	Sea Green, light
■	991	Aquamarine, dark
♥	992	Aquamarine, medium
☆	993	Aquamarine, light
⬕	3685	Mauve, dark
✚	3687	Mauve
m	3688	Mauve, medium
⊥	3689	Mauve, light
3	3803	Mauve, medium dark
⬎	3814	Aquamarine

Backstitch Instructions

Yellow-green leaves: DMC® 561 Jade, very dark.

Blue-green leaves: DMC® 991 Aquamarine, dark.

Stems and curlicues: DMC® 898 Coffee Brown, very dark.

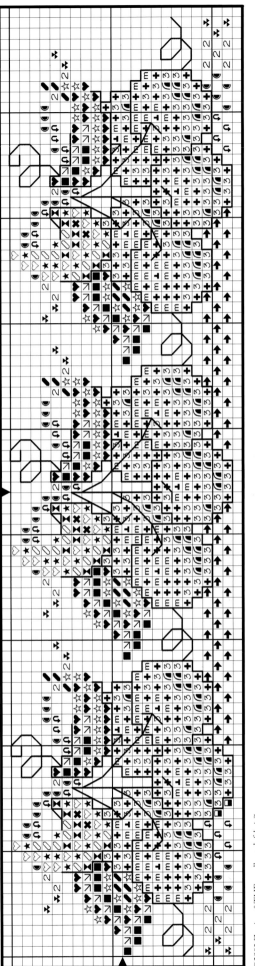

©2003 Zweigart® THE needlework fabric™

Cross Stitch: 3 strands
Backstitch: 1 strand
French Knots: 1 strand
  wrapped twice
Stitch Count: 30 wide x 30
  high (spring, summer,
  and autumn)
  29 wide x 30 high (winter)
**Approximate Finished Size
(11-count):**
  2⅝" square (each design)

Supplies

- DMC® 11-count White Aida
- DMC® 6-Strand
  Embroidery Floss
  - 1 skein each #310, #367,
    #666, #725, #727, #746,
    #801, #809, #818, #891,
    #913, #954, #955, #956,
    #957, #3341, #3747,
    #3864
- 4 Crafter's Pride Acrylic
  Round Coasters
- #24 Tapestry Needle

Four Seasons Coasters

Designs by Roberta Madeleine
Stitching by Lois Hiles

*Your coasters will always be in season with this coaster set. Each season features a
bird and decorative wreath that is mounted in an acrylic round coaster. The coaster
set is an ideal gift—inexpensive and useful. And for the stitcher, the designs are not at
all cumbersome.*

General Instructions

1. Complete all cross stitch and backstitch.
2. Do the French knots.
3. Trim the stitched pieces to fit within each coaster.
4. Follow the manufacturer's instructions for finishing
   the coasters.

Backstitch Instructions

Stems: DMC® 367 Pistachio Green, dark.

Berries (winter wreath): DMC® 666 Christmas Red,
bright.

All other backstitch: DMC® 801 Coffee Brown, dark.

DMC® 6-Strand Embroidery Floss*

◥	310	Black	□	809	Delft Blue	L	956	Geranium
■	367	Pistachio Green, dark	/	818	Baby Pink	<	957	Geranium, pale
▲	666	Christmas Red, bright	⊥	891	Carnation, dark	▲	3341	Apricot
✚	725	Topaz	○	913	Nile Green, medium	♥	3747	Blue Violet, very light
√	727	Topaz, very light	△	954	Nile Green, medium	☆	3864	Mocha Beige, light
ට	746	Off-White	♡	955	Nile Green, light			

Colors and symbols for all four charts, but not every color/symbol appears in each chart.

French Knot Instructions

Winter Wreath
- Berries: DMC® 666 Christmas Red, bright.
- Cardinal's eye: DMC® 727 Topaz, very light.

Spring Wreath
- Berries: DMC® 956 Geranium.
- Robin's eye: DMC® 310 Black.

Summer Wreath
- Berries: DMC® 809 Delft Blue.
- Bluebird's eye: DMC® 310 Black.

Autumn Wreath
- Berries: DMC® 957 Geranium, pale.
- Yellow bird's eye: DMC® 310 Black.

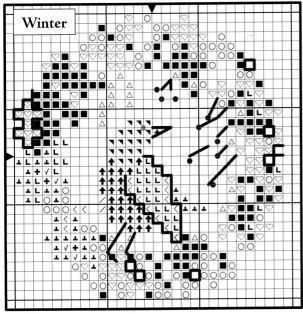

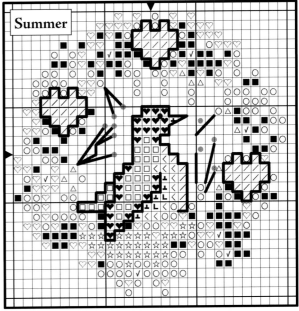

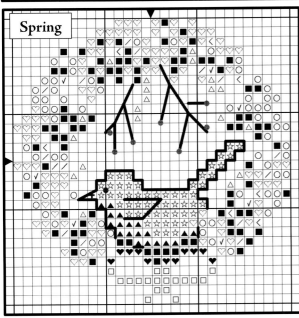

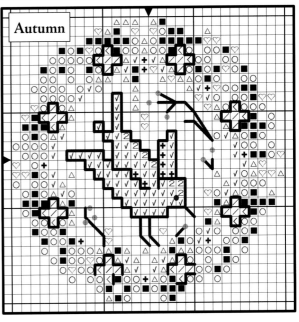

Cross Stitch: 3 strands
Backstitch: 1 strand
Stitch Count: 93 wide x 48 high
Approximate Finished Size
   (11-count): 8½" x 4⅜"

Supplies

- Sudberry House Small Tea Tray #80031
- DMC® 11-count White Aida
- DMC® 6-Strand Embroidery Floss
  - 1 skein each #367, #913, #962, #963, #3716, #3831, #3840
- #24 Tapestry Needle

Teatime Tea Tray

Design by Roberta Madeleine
Stitching by Lois Hiles

Teatime will never be the same once you've served tea on this terrific tray. Stitched on 11-count, this is a quick-to-stitch project. The design, mounted in Sudberry's rich mahogany small tea tray embellished with brass handles, makes a wonderful gift that is sure to be welcomed by any recipient.

DMC® 6-Strand Embroidery Floss

- ● 367   Pistachio Green, dark
- ✚ 913   Nile Green, medium
- ◢ 962   Dusty Rose, medium
- △ 963   Dusty Rose, ultra very light
- ★ 3716   Dusty Rose, very light
- □ 3840   Lavender Blue, light

Backstitch Instructions

Roses: DMC® 3831 Raspberry, dark.

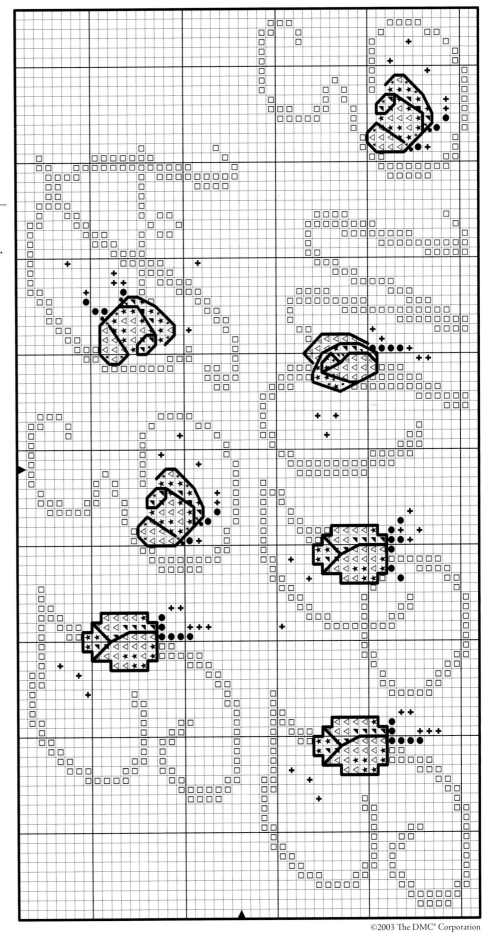

Cross Stitch: 3 strands
Backstitch: 1 strand (2 strands on lettering)
French Knots: 2 strands wrapped twice
Stitch Count: 94 wide x 108 high
Approximate Finished Size (11-count):
  8½" x 9¾"

Supplies

- Adam Original Prefinished Album Cover with Zweigart® 11-count Antique White Pearl Aida
- DMC® 6-Strand Embroidery Floss
  - 1 skein each White, #153, #154, #310, #317, #413, #414, #433, #434, #435, #436, #437, #772, #783, #801, #895, #3078, #3345, #3346, #3347, #3348, #3799, #3820, #3821, #3822, #3823, #3834, #3835, #3836
- 1 skein DMC® #30955 6-Strand Rayon Floss*
- 1 package Mill Hill® #10074 Purple Passion Magnifica Beads
- #24 Tapestry Needle
- Beading Needle
- 10½"-wide Photo Album

*May be substituted with DMC® #955 6-Strand Embroidery Floss.

Our Family Memories Album Cover

Design by Pamela Kellogg
Stitching by Kim Dennett

Add pizzazz to your photo album with a cross stitched prefinished album cover. A Monarch butterfly takes a rest among daisies and dark plum berries, accented with Purple Passion Magnifica glass beads. This album cover adjusts to different sizes. It can expand to fit an album approximately 14" wide. The design shown here was centered with 17 blank rows on top and bottom and 14 blank rows on the right and left sides to fit a 10½"-wide album cover. To fit a larger cover up, place the design on the album to locate the total stitching area and then locate the center of the fabric.

Chart continued on next page.

• Because rayon floss is slippery and knots easily, use shorter strands (approximately 12" long). Moistening the floss with water as you stitch further helps to eliminate kinks.

• If preferred, you may substitute beads with French knots using DMC® 3834 Grape, dark.

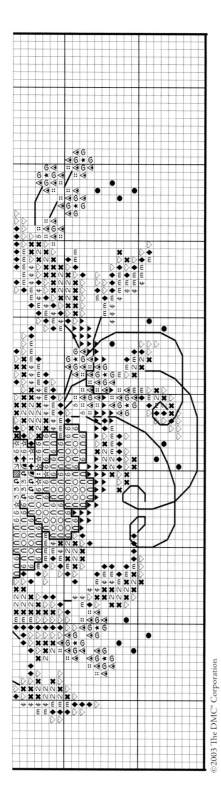

DMC® 6-Strand Embroidery Floss

O	White	White
★	153	Lavender, light
8	154	Plum, dark
■	310	Black
4	317	Pewter Gray
X	413	Pewter Gray, dark
◢	414	Steel Gray, dark
↘	433	Brown, medium
→	434	Brown, light
◖	435	Brown, very light
∩	436	Tan
3	437	Tan, light
2	772	Yellow Green, very light
♥	783	Topaz, medium
▨	801	Coffee Brown, dark
¢	895	Hunter Green, very dark

6	3078	Golden Yellow, very light
m	3345	Hunter Green, dark
◆	3346	Hunter Green
♡	3347	Yellow Green, medium
✖	3348	Yellow Green, light
Z	3799	Pewter Gray, very dark
//	3820	Straw, dark
:	3821	Straw
☆	3822	Straw, light
∩	3823	Yellow, very pale
::	3834	Grape, dark
⋀	3835	Grape, medium
ၜ	3836	Grape, light

DMC® 6-Strand Rayon Floss

▼	30955	Nile Green, light

Backstitch Instructions

Berries: DMC® 154 Plum, dark.
Butterfly: DMC® 310 Black (one strand).
Lettering: DMC® 310 Black (two strands).
Leaves: DMC® 895 Hunter Green, very dark.
Daisies: DMC® 3820 Straw, dark.

French Knot Instructions

● Butterfly's antennae: DMC® 310 Black.

Bead Instructions

● Attach Mill Hill® 10074 Purple Passion Magnifica glass beads with two strands DMC® White embroidery floss. Refer to the "Attaching Beads" section in the General Instructions, page 138, for further assistance, if necessary.

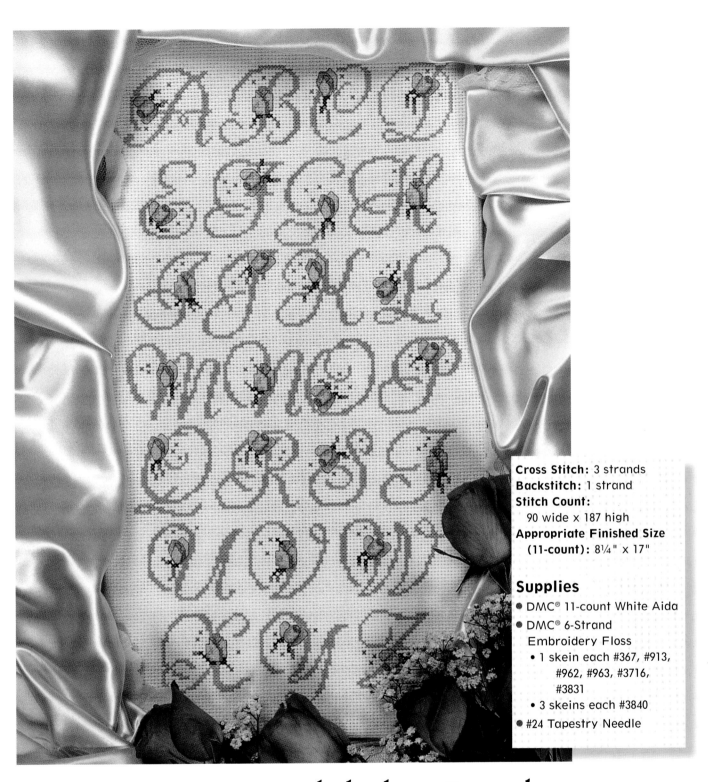

Cross Stitch: 3 strands
Backstitch: 1 strand
Stitch Count:
  90 wide x 187 high
**Appropriate Finished Size
(11-count):** 8¼" x 17"

Supplies

- DMC® 11-count White Aida
- DMC® 6-Strand
  Embroidery Floss
  - 1 skein each #367, #913,
    #962, #963, #3716,
    #3831
  - 3 skeins each #3840
- #24 Tapestry Needle

Victorian Alphabet Sampler

Design by Roberta Madeleine
Stitching by Lois Hiles

Embellish a piece with the Victorian elegance of miniature rosebuds and a monogram. You'll love working with these letters, as they take less than an hour to stitch per letter. Ideas for personalized projects include blouses or shirts like the denim Rose-Monogrammed Shirt (page 131), sweatshirts, coasters, bookmarks, mugs, checkbook covers, and more.

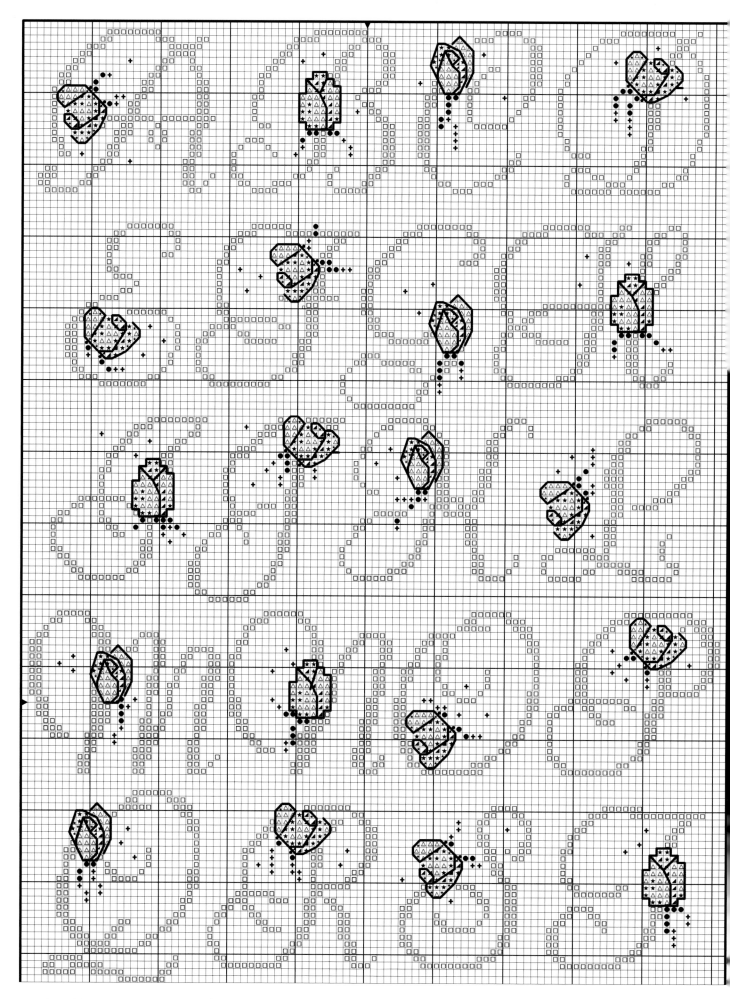

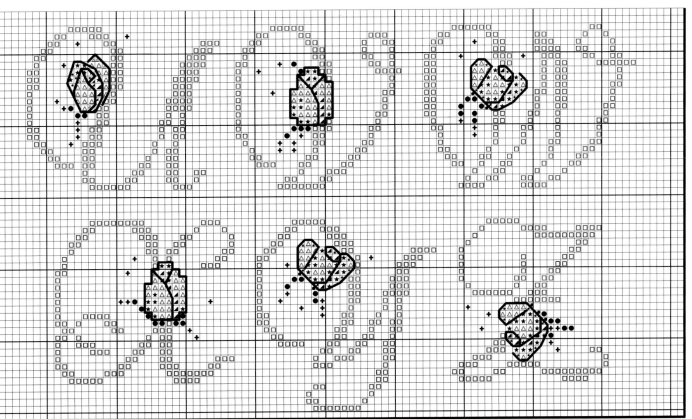

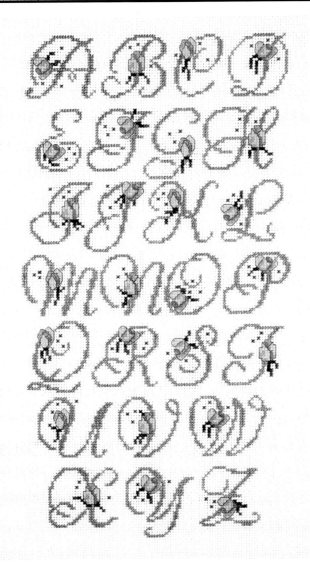

DMC® 6-Strand Embroidery Floss

●	367	Pistachio Green, dark
+	913	Nile Green, medium
◢	962	Dusty Rose, medium
△	963	Dusty Rose, ultra very light
★	3716	Dusty Rose, very light
□	3840	Lavender Blue, light

Backstitch Instructions

Roses: DMC® 3831 Raspberry, dark.

Easy See, Easy Stitch

Friendship

Flowers in the Garden of Life
Framed Verse and Afghan

Designs by Mike Vickery
Stitching by Julie Woodard (afghan) and Lois Hiles (framed verse)

Truly, friends are the flowers in the garden of life ... each friend being unique as each flower is different. Each friend is a blessing to appreciate and respect. This afghan is a wonderful display of how much your friend's relationship means to you. If you don't have time to stitch the afghan, you have several options with this project—stitch the friendship verse with floral design, stitch only the friendship verse, or stitch one of the flowers—and finish as a framed picture or pillow.

Cross Stitch: 3 strands
Backstitch: 1 strand
French Knots: 2 strands
                       wrapped twice
Stitch Count: 72 wide x 72 high
Approximate Finished Size
   (11-count): 6½" square

Supplies

- DMC® 11-count White Aida
- DMC® 6-Strand Embroidery Floss
  - 1 skein each #208, #210, #211,
    #317, #322, #498, #720, #721,
    #722, #725, #727, #783, #797,
    #890, #910, #912, #954, #3755
- #24 Tapestry Needle

Framed Verse

The piece shown here was stitched with three strands and backstitched with one strand. Another option would be to cross stitch with four strands and backstitch with two strands—the same as the afghan. Using fewer strands results in a lighter overall effect, while more strands yield a darker and fuller stitch throughout. Use the number of strands to yield what you prefer to be the result.

Backstitch Instructions

Lettering: DMC® 797 Royal Blue.

Heart: DMC® 498 Christmas Red.

Border and all other backstitch: DMC® 317 Pewter Gray.

French Knots

- Lettering: DMC® 797 Royal Blue.

DMC® 6-Strand Embroidery Floss

←	208	Lavender, very dark		L	727	Topaz, very light
+	210	Lavender, medium		▼	783	Topaz, medium
C	211	Lavender, light		↑	797	Royal Blue
$	322	Baby Blue, dark		●	890	Pistachio Green, ultra dark
⩗	720	Orange Spice, dark		⊕	910	Emerald Green, dark
8	721	Orange Spice, medium		//	912	Emerald Green, light
H	722	Orange Spice, light		)	954	Nile Green
⋘	725	Topaz		2	3755	Baby Blue

DMC® 6-Strand Embroidery Floss

↑ 797 Royal Blue
⊕ **910** Emerald Green, dark

Backstitch Instructions
Lettering: DMC® 797 Royal Blue.
Heart: DMC® 498 Christmas Red.
Border and all other backstitch: DMC® 317 Pewter Gray.

French Knots
● Lettering: DMC® 797 Royal Blue.

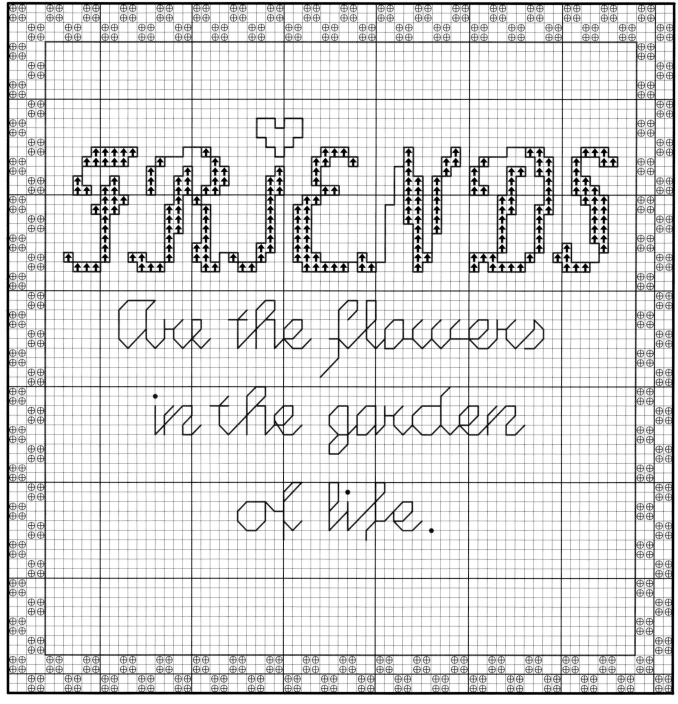

Cross Stitch: 4 strands
Backstitch: 2 strands
French Knots: 2 strands wrapped three times
Stitch Counts: 72 wide x 72 high (each design)
Approximate Finished Size (11-count): 6½" square (each design)

Supplies

- Zweigart® 11-count Antique White Merino Afghan (Four rows across and seven rows down results in 28 squares total.)
- DMC® 6-Strand Embroidery Floss
  - 1 skein each #208, #210, #211, # 322, #327, #350, #352, #375, #498, #720, #721, #722, #783, #817, #890, #962, #963, #3078, #3325, #3716, #3755, #3856
  - 2 skeins each #725, #727
  - 3 skeins each #317, #912, #954
  - 5 skeins #797
  - 15 skeins #910
- #24 Tapestry Needle

Friends (with flowers)

Red Rose

Iris

Friends (with flowers)

Pink Daisy

Friends (no flowers)

Friends (no flowers)

Lily

Friends (no flowers)

Daffodil

Aster

Friends (no flowers)

Friends (with flowers)

Friends (no flowers)

Friends (with flowers)

Friends (no flowers)

Friends (no flowers)

Iris

Pink Daisy

Friends (no flowers)

Lily

Friends (no flowers)

Friends (no flowers)

Aster

Friends (with flowers)

Daffodil

Red Rose

Friends (with flowers)

Afghan Layout

General Instructions

The 11-count Merino afghan contains four rows across and seven rows down. Follow layout on the previous page to stitch all squares as the model is shown. If you prefer a quicker afghan to stitch using these same designs, refer to the two other options provided below.

When cross stitch is completed, fringe as desired.

Other Design Layout Options for Afghan

On the previous page, you will find the complete layout used for the friendship afghan. Here are two more options that use fewer squares for quicker stitching.

Option 1 (10 of 28 squares stitched)

For this look, each flower motif is stitched once, the "Friends …" with the flowers motif is stitched twice, and the "Friends …" without flowers motif is stitched twice. Here's how it all comes together (working left to right and top to bottom):

Top Row: Stitch the rose motif in the top left square, skip two squares, and stitch the iris in top right square.

Second Row: Skip a square, stitch the "Friends …" with flowers motif in the second square, and leave the last two squares blank.

Third Row: Skip first two squares, stitch "Friends …" without flowers motif in the third square, and leave the last square blank.

Fourth Row: Stitch the daisy motif in first square, skip the next two squares, and stitch the lily in the fourth square.

Fifth Row: Skip the first square, stitch the "Friends …" without flowers motif in the second square, and leave the last two squares blank.

Sixth Row: Skip the first two squares, stitch the "Friends …" with flowers motif in the third square, and leave the last square blank.

Bottom Row: Stitch the daffodil motif in the first square, skip two squares, and stitch the aster motif in the fourth square.

Option 2 (14 of 28 squares stitched)

For this layout, the rose, daisy, iris, and "Friends …" without flowers blocks are stitched twice, the "Friends …" with flowers motif is stitched three times, and the daffodil and lily motifs are stitched once. Here's how it comes together:

Top Row: Stitch the "Friends …" with flowers motif in the top left square, skip a square, stitch the rose motif in the third square, and leave the fourth square blank.

Second Row: Skip the first square, stitch the iris motif in the second square, skip the third square, and stitch the "Friends …" without flowers motif in the fourth square.

Third Row: Stitch the daisy motif in the first square, skip the second square, stitch the lily motif in the third square, and leave the fourth square blank.

Fourth Row: Skip the first square, stitch the "Friends …" with flowers motif in the second square, skip the third square, and stitch the daffodil motif in the fourth square.

Fifth Row: Stitch the "Friends …" without flowers motif in the first square, skip a square, stitch the aster motif in the third square, and leave the fourth square blank.

Sixth Row: Skip the first square, stitch the rose motif in the second square, skip a square, and stitch the "Friends …" with flowers motif in the fourth square.

Bottom Row: Stitch the iris motif in the first square, skip a square, stitch the daisy motif in the third square, and leave the fourth square blank.

Red Rose

DMC® 6-Strand Embroidery Floss

⋘	350	Coral, medium	⊕	910	Emerald Green, dark
√	352	Coral, light	//	912	Emerald Green, light
♥	498	Christmas Red, dark	)	954	Nile Green
★	817	Coral Red, very dark			

Backstitch Instructions

All backstitch: DMC® 317 Pewter Gray.

Iris

DMC® 6-Strand Embroidery Floss

←	208	Lavender, very dark	L	727	Topaz, very light
+	210	Lavender, medium	▼	783	Topaz, medium
C	211	Lavender, light	⊕	910	Emerald Green, dark
■	327	Violet, very dark	//	912	Emerald Green, light
⋘	725	Topaz	)	954	Nile Green

Backstitch Instructions

All backstitch: DMC® 317 Pewter Gray.

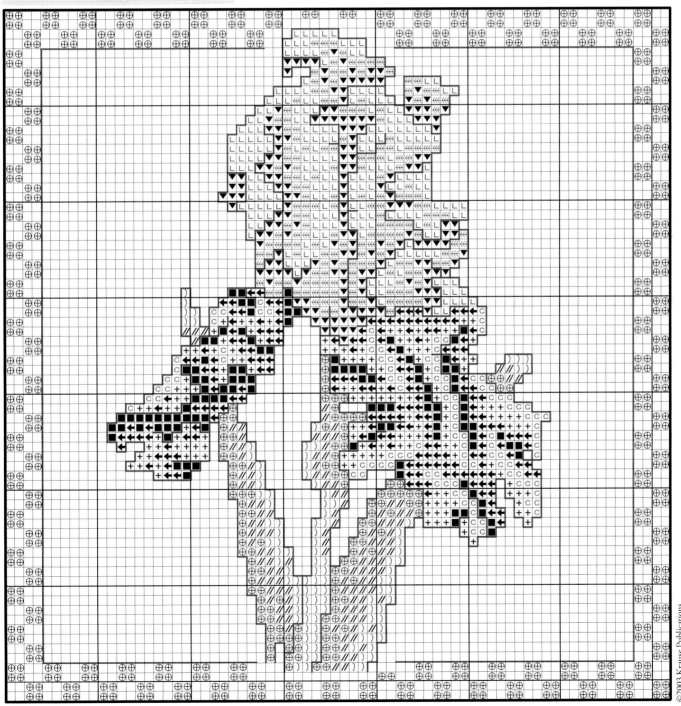

Lily

DMC® 6-Strand Embroidery Floss

⚠	720	Orange Spice, dark	//	912	Emerald Green, light
8	721	Orange Spice, medium	)	954	Nile Green
H	722	Orange Spice, light	T	3856	Mahogany,
⊕	910	Emerald Green, dark			ultra very light

Backstitch Instructions

All backstitch: DMC® 317 Pewter Gray.

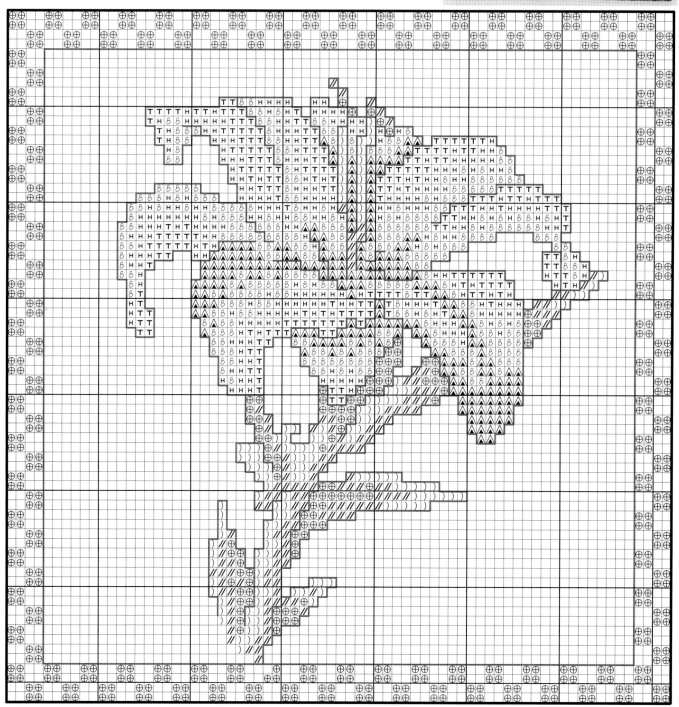

Blue Aster

DMC® 6-Strand Embroidery Floss

$	322	Baby Blue, dark	//	912	Emerald Green, light
≪	725	Topaz	)	954	Nile Green
L	727	Topaz, very light	n	3325	Baby Blue, light
↑	797	Royal Blue	2	3755	Baby Blue
⊕	910	Emerald Green, dark			

Backstitch Instructions

All backstitch: DMC® 317 Pewter Gray.

Daffodil

DMC® 6-Strand Embroidery Floss

⫶⫶⫶	725	Topaz	//	912	Emerald Green, light	
L	727	Topaz, very light	)	954	Nile Green	
▼	783	Topaz, medium	:	3078	Golden Yellow,	
⊕	910	Emerald Green, dark			very light	

Backstitch Instructions

All backstitch: DMC® 317 Pewter Gray.

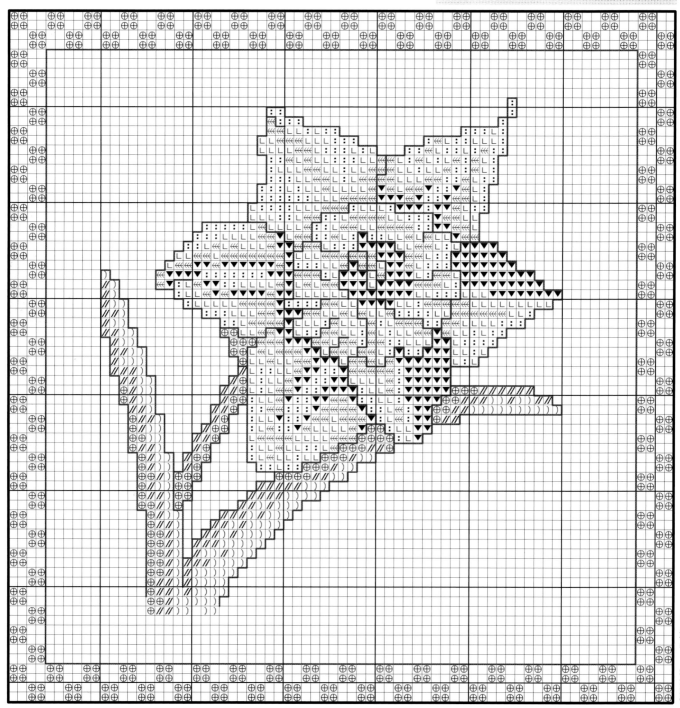

©2003 Krause Publications

Pink Daisy

DMC® 6-Strand Embroidery Floss

⫷ 725	Topaz	
▼ 783	Topaz, medium	
⊕ 910	Emerald Green, dark	
// 912	Emerald Green, light	
) 954	Nile Green	

✿ 962	Dusty Rose, medium
— 963	Dusty Rose, ultra very light
✤ 3716	Dusty Rose, very light

Backstitch Instructions

All backstitch: DMC® 317 Pewter Gray.

Cross Stitch: 3 strands
Backstitch: 1 strand
Stitch Count: 76 wide x 98 high
Approximate Finished Size
  (11-count): 6⅞" x 8⅞"

Supplies
- Zweigart® 11-count Beige Aida
- Anchor® 6-Strand Embroidery Floss
  - 1 skein each #1, #6, #8, #48, #49, #50, #109, #136, #137, #158, #159, #211, #225, #241, #265, #292, #293, #342, #359, #360, #368, #390, #846, #848, #874, #926, #1044
- #24 Tapestry Needle

The Path Sampler

Design by Roberta Madeleine

Friendships are just one of God's many gifts to us. Each friendship is unique in its own special way. So, whether you travel by flying, sailing, driving, or walking, the trip to see a friend is never too long. This sampler would be a nice gift to your friend for his/her hospitality and as a reminder of your special bond.

Anchor® 6-Strand Embroidery Floss

√	1	Snow White	○	158	Sapphire, very light	●	359	Coffee, medium
★	6	Salmon, very light	Z	159	Sapphire, light	–	368	Spice, medium light
T	8	Salmon, light	✎	211	Spruce, medium dark	◢	390	Linen, light
2	48	China Rose, very light	⊥	225	Emerald, light	▼	846	Fern Green, dark
✖	49	China Rose, light	♡	241	Grass Green	∧	848	Blue Mist
☆	50	China Rose, medium	L	265	Avocado, light	4	874	Saffron, medium
□	109	Lavender, medium light	|	292	Jonquil, very light	△	926	Ecru, very light
↑	136	Wedgwood, light	+	293	Jonquil, light	■	1044	Grass Green, ultra dark
/	137	Wedgwood, medium	♥	342	Lilac, light			

Backstitch Instructions
Lettering: Anchor® 359 Coffee, medium.
All other backstitch: Anchor® 360 Coffee, very dark.

The path to a
friend's house is
never too long.

Easy See, Easy Stitch for

Special Events

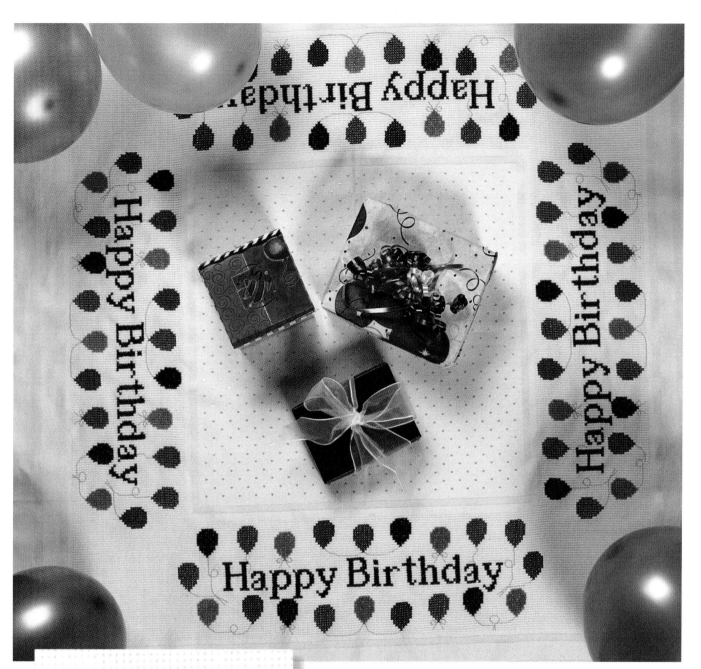

Cross Stitch: 3 strands
Backstitch: 2 strands
Stitch Count: 158 wide x 49 high
Approximate Finished Size
  (10-count): 15⅞" x 5"

Supplies

- Zweigart® Prefinished 10-count White Largo Table Topper
- DMC® 6-Strand Embroidery Floss
  - 1 skein each #415, #552, #726, #825, #911
  - 7 skeins #321
- #24 Tapestry Needle

Happy Birthday Table Topper

Design by Phyllis Dobbs
Stitching by Wanda Webster

Birthday celebrations become even more special with this festive birthday table topper. It's perfect for adults and children—a birthday tradition to be enjoyed for generations. You don't have to construct this table topper. Just cross stitch on the 10-count Aida insert of the prefinished table topper and your project is complete.

General Instructions

Stitch the complete motif centered on all four sides of the table topper. Refer to the specific instructions on the chart for the actual starting place for the stitching.

Backstitch Instructions

Balloon strings: DMC® 415 Pearl Gray.

DMC® 6-Strand Embroidery Floss

▲	321	Christmas Red
↓	552	Violet, medium
✚	726	Topaz, light
■	825	Blue, dark
●	911	Emerald Green, medium

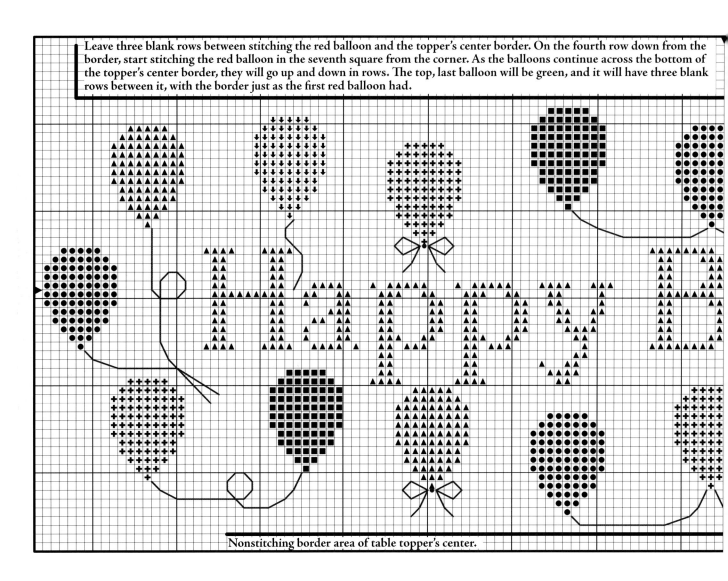

Leave three blank rows between stitching the red balloon and the topper's center border. On the fourth row down from the border, start stitching the red balloon in the seventh square from the corner. As the balloons continue across the bottom of the topper's center border, they will go up and down in rows. The top, last balloon will be green, and it will have three blank rows between it, with the border just as the first red balloon had.

Nonstitching border area of table topper's center.

Leave three blank rows between stitching the red balloon and the topper's center border. On the fourth row down from the border, start stitching the red balloon in the seventh square from the corner. As the balloons continue across the bottom of the topper's center border, they will go up and down in rows. The top, last balloon will be green, and it will have three blank rows between it, with the border just as the first red balloon had.

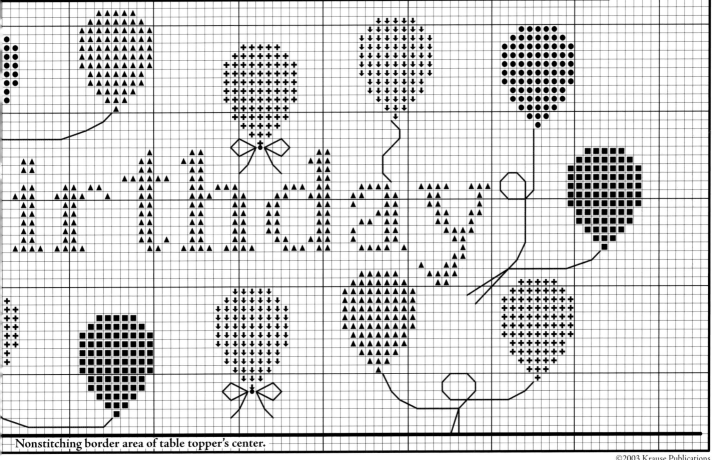

Nonstitching border area of table topper's center.

©2003 Krause Publications

The cross-stitch design in the frame reads:

Reach for the Stars
CONGRATULATIONS
Name
Name
Month Date Year

Cross Stitch: 3 strands
Backstitch: 2 strands
Stitch Count: 77 wide x 100 high
Approximate Finished Size (11-count): 7" x 9"

Supplies

- Charles Craft 11-count White Aida
- Anchor® 6-Strand Embroidery Floss
  - 1 skein each #2, #46, #305
  - 3 skeins #133
- 1 spool Kreinik Blending Filament High Lustre™ #002HL
- Mill Hill® Opal Glass Star Treasure #12174
- Mill Hill® Red Glass Star Treasure #12172
- Mill Hill® Blue Glass Star Treasure #12173
- 8½" x 11" Frame
- #24 Tapestry Needle

Star Instructions

The white backstitched stars go in the blue border. Three red backstitched stars go to the left of "Reach" and three red ones go to the right of "Reach." Three blue backstitched stars go to the left of "Stars" and another three blue backstitched stars go to the right of "Stars." For further clarification, refer to photograph.

Anchor® 6-Strand Embroidery Floss

⊥	2	White
◥	46	Crimson Red
△	133	Cobalt Blue, dark

Kreinik Blending Filament High Lustre™

Blended needle of two strands High Lustre™ and one strand Anchor® floss.

●	002HL	Kreinik Gold and
	305	Anchor® Topaz, light

Mill Hill® Glass Star Treasures

★	12172	Red
■	12173	Blue
♥	12174	Opal

Graduation Sampler

Design by Roberta Madeleine
Stitching by Susan Banbury

Commemorate the graduate's special event with this sampler, encouraging him or her to "Reach for the Stars." The patriotic theme, complete with red, white, and blue glass stars, is a reminder that we have the freedom to learn and to grow intellectually.

Try a few other options for the stars.
Option 1: Replace the backstitched stars with Star Treasures for a really sparkling sampler with great dimension.
Option 2: Replace the Star Treasures with backstitched stars.
Option 3: Have all of the stars within the main area be Star Treasures and the stars in the blue border be backstitched.
If you use the glass stars and plan to have the project framed with glass, you will need to have either a raised mat or spacers. A professional framer will know how to achieve what is best for your project.

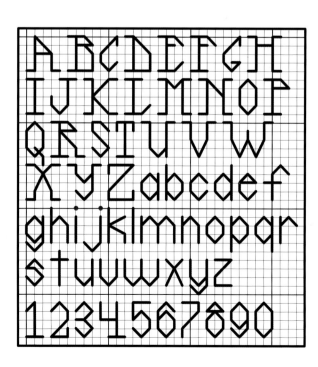

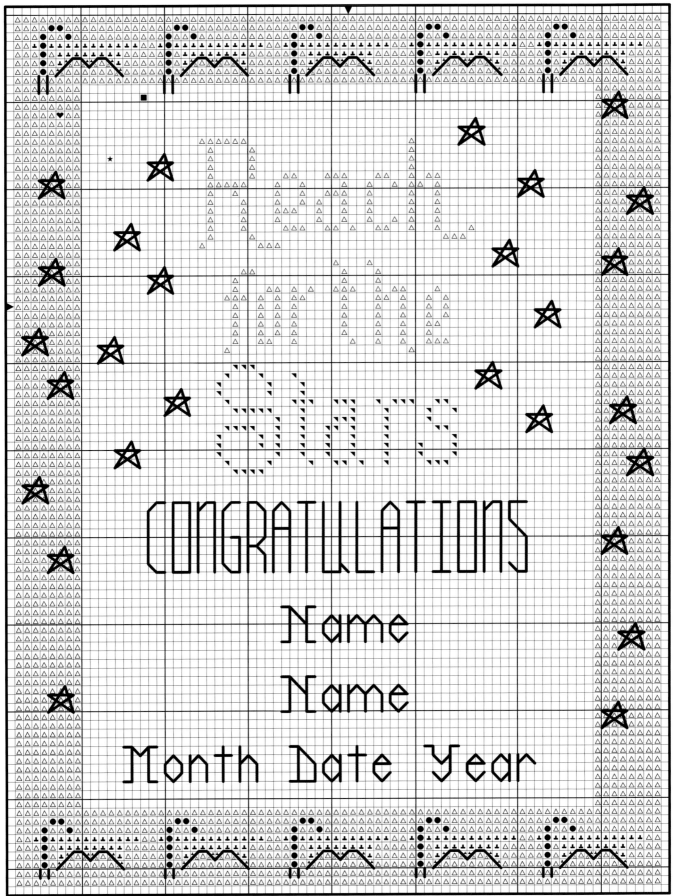

©2003 Anchor®

Cross Stitch: 1 strand
(#3 pearl cotton)
Backstitch: 3 strands
(6-strand embroidery floss)
Stitch Count:
58 wide x 62 high
**Approximate Finished Size
(7-count):** 8¼" x 8⅞"

Supplies

- Beautiful Accents™ Prefinished Table Topper made with Zweigart® 7-count Black Country Aida
- Anchor® #3 Pearl Cotton
  - 1 skein each #2, #145, #302, #303, #304, #368, #369, #370, #372, #399, #403
- Anchor® 6-Strand Embroidery Floss
  - 1 skein each #400, #403
- #22 Tapestry Needle

Halloween Bear Table Topper

Design by Mike Vickery
Stitching by Jessica Milidonis

With his costume of a cape and mask, this bear is ready for his trick-or-treat bag to be filled with Halloween goodies. This cute bear in his brightly colored vest against the black Country Aida table topper sets the stage for a fun Halloween night ... and many more in years to come.

tips

• You might find it easier to start stitching this design from the bottom of the design up to ensure the proper space is left between the bottom of the design and the beginning of the fringe area. Another suggestion is to also count stitches on each side and mark with a pin to determine if you have the design centered before you actually start stitching.

• If substituting 6-strand embroidery floss for the #3 pearl cotton, you would use the same color numbers and stitch with four strands.

General Instructions

Measure 22 rows up from the basting row of fringe of the table topper's center point and mark with a pin. This represents the row of the bottom of the design. From that row, measure in on each side of basting row approximately 3". The design should be centered within that area.

Backstitch Instructions

Use Anchor® 6-Strand Embroidery Floss for the backstitch.
"Trick or Treat": Anchor® 403 Black.
All other backstitch: Anchor® 400 Gray, medium.

Anchor® #3 Pearl Cotton

·	2	White
√	145	Delft Blue, light
∕	302	Citrus, medium light
8	303	Citrus, medium
←	304	Citrus, dark
2	368	Spice, medium light
$	369	Spice, medium
▲	370	Spice, medium dark
✳	372	Desert, light
#	399	Gray, medium
●	403	Black

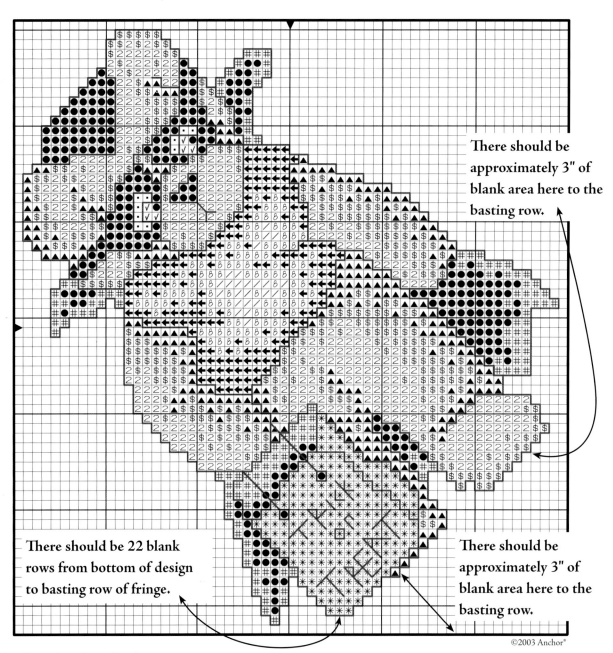

There should be approximately 3" of blank area here to the basting row.

There should be 22 blank rows from bottom of design to basting row of fringe.

There should be approximately 3" of blank area here to the basting row.

©2003 Anchor®

Easy See, Easy Stitch
Wearables

Cross Stitch: 1 strand (#3 Pearl Cotton)
Backstitch: 1 strand (#5 Pearl Cotton)
French Knots: 6 strands (floss)
 wrapped once
Stitch Count: 91 wide x 91 high
Approximate Finished Size (7-count):
  13" square

Supplies

- Beautiful Accents™ Prefinished Shawl
  made with Zweigart®
  7-count Black Country Aida
- Anchor® #3 Pearl Cotton
  - 1 skein each #2, #8, #25, #28, #46, #96,
     #167, #169, #240, #243, #246, #254,
     #288, #301, #302, #304, #339
- 1 skein #403 Anchor® #5 Pearl Cotton
- 1 skein #28 Anchor®
  6-Strand Embroidery Floss
- #22 Tapestry Needle

Hawaiian Floral Shawl

Design by Roberta Madeleine
Stitching by Susan Banbury

Multicolored tropical flowers everywhere you look, the cool breeze from the ocean's waves, sand around your feet, fresh pineapple from the fields ... all this and more when you visit Hawaii. Whether this shawl is reminiscent of your visit to a tropical island paradise or a dream to visit such a spectacular place, you'll be the center of attention with this colorful drape. The ultra softness of the Country Aida makes the shawl perfect for those cool summer evenings. You'll also love how quickly the shawl stitches up on the 7-count.

General Instructions

Read these instructions carefully before stitching so that motifs fit properly on the shawl. There are options given for motif placements.

1. To find the center of the shawl, fold the shawl in half along the long diagonal edge.
2. Mark the center with a pin.
3. Stitch the large motif centered on shawl approximately 23 squares down from the top of the shawl. (Note: The stitched model shown was only five squares from the top of the shawl. By allowing 23 squares between the top of the shawl and the beginning of the main motif, it automatically moves the border motif closer to the edges of the shawl where it will better represent the design on the shawl. This also allows for the top of the shawl to be draped somewhat without interfering with the design elements.)

Border Instructions

1. When the main motif is completed, measure 23 diagonal spaces down from the bottom center of the main motif.
2. The corner border motif should be stitched first. Refer to the close-up photograph for clarification.

3. Stitch the horizontal border, leaving one space between motifs. Leave 23 spaces between the main motif and border. Repeat about seven times to line the border up with the top of the main motif.
4. Stitch the vertical border, leaving one space between motifs. Leave 23 spaces between the main motif and the border. Repeat about seven times to line up the vertical border with the top of the main motif.
5. Fringe the stitched shawl.

♥	2	White
□	8	Salmon, light
2	25	Carnation, light
⊥	28	Carnation, medium dark
○	46	Crimson Red
∧	96	Violet, light

Anchor® #3 Pearl Cotton

∟	167	Surf Blue, very light
△	169	Surf Blue, medium
T	240	Grass Green, light
◢	243	Grass Green, medium
↑	246	Grass Green, very dark
♡	254	Parrot Green, light

◢	288	Canary Yellow, light
│	301	Citrus
=	302	Citrus, medium light
●	304	Citrus, dark
▲	339	Terra Cotta, medium

Backstitch Instructions

All backstitch: Anchor® 403
#5 Pearl Cotton, Black.

French Knot Instructions

● Pistil of yellow flower: Anchor® 288 6-Strand Embroidery Floss,
Canary Yellow, light.

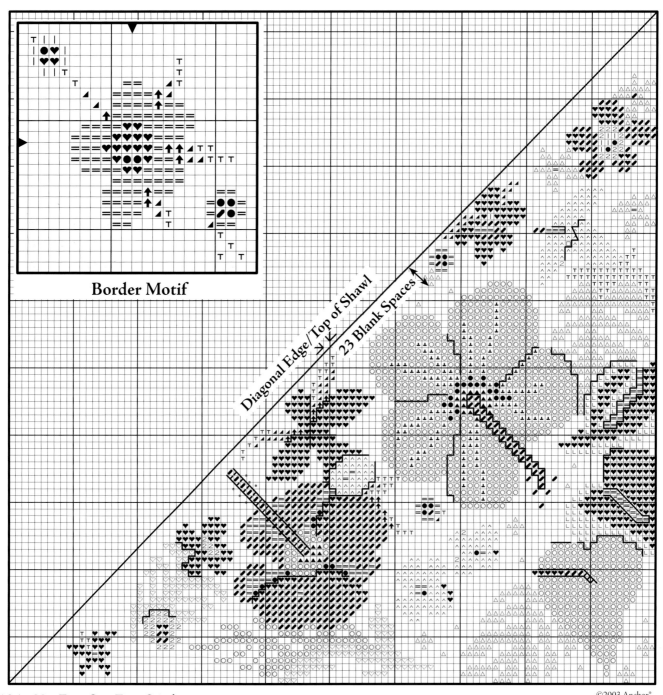

Border Motif

©2003 Anchor®

Cross Stitch: 6 strands (each design)
Backstitch: 2 strands (each design)
French Knots: 3 strands wrapped twice (each design)
Stitch Count: 44 wide x 80 high (each design)
Approximate Finished Size
  (7-count): 6¼" x 11½" (each design)

Supplies

- Adam Original Prefinished Adult Vest with Zwegart® 7-count Cream Klostern
- DMC® 6-Strand Embroidery Floss
  - 1 skein each White, #309, #310, #317, #413, #414, #561, #562, #563, #564, #783, #813, #824, #825, #826, #827, #828, #955, #3078, #3799, #3820, #3821, #3822, #3823
- #24 Tapestry Needle

Morning Glory Vests

Design by Pamela Kellogg
Stitching by Lois Hiles

Butterflies flutter around trumpet-shaped morning glories on a vest that can be worn with jeans, khakis, skirts, and dresses. The 7-count Klostern vest is shown in two colors—sand and cream—which are colors that will coordinate with everything. The weight of the fabric makes this vest perfect for those cool summer evenings through the briskness of autumn.

Due to the loose weave in the fabric, it is recommended that a hoop should not be used with this prefinished product.

Morning Glory Vest

DMC® 6-Strand Embroidery Floss

o	White	White
●	310	Black
⊘	317	Pewter Gray
➜	413	Pewter Gray, dark
△	414	Steel Gray, dark
■	561	Jade, very dark
♡	562	Jade, medium
✗	563	Jade, light
¢	564	Jade, very light
✚	783	Topaz, medium
☆	813	Blue, light
2	825	Blue, dark
♥	826	Blue, medium
⌒	827	Blue, very light
4	828	Blue, ultra very light
◢	955	Nile Green, light
★	3078	Golden Yellow, very light
∩	3799	Pewter Gray, very dark
3	3820	Straw, dark
∷	3821	Straw
//	3822	Straw, light
m	3823	Yellow, very pale

Backstitch Instructions

Pink lines on morning glories: DMC® 309 Rose, deep.
Butterfly: DMC® 310 Black.
Vines: DMC® 561 Jade, very dark.
Morning glories: DMC® 824 Blue, very dark.

Left side

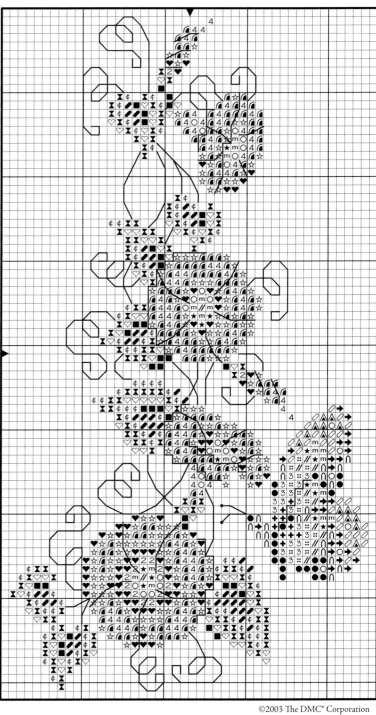

©2003 The DMC® Corporation

The keycode, backstitch, and French knot instructions are the same for both the left and right sides.

(Left Side)

French Knot Instructions

- Butterfly antennae: DMC® 310 Black.

Right side

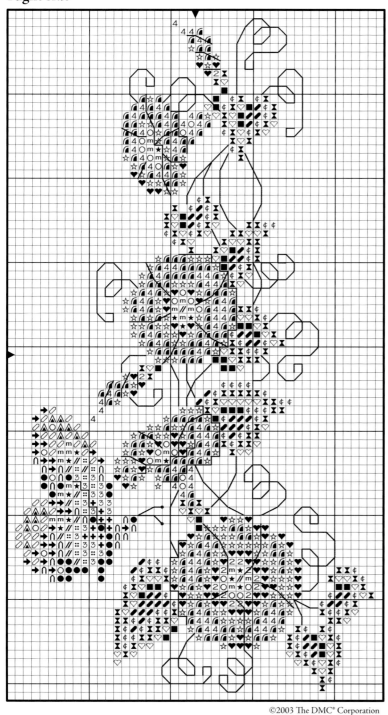

©2003 The DMC® Corporation

(Right Side)

Backstitch: 6 strands (embroidery floss) or 1 strand (#3 pearl cotton)

Supplies

- Zweigart® 11-count Antique White Wool Aida
- 1 skein Anchor® #403 6-Strand Embroidery Floss
- 1 skein Anchor® #799 #3 Pearl Cotton
- #22 Tapestry Needle (embroidery floss)
- #20 Tapestry Needle (#3 pearl cotton)

Monogrammed Winter Scarf

Design by Mike Vickery

Centuries ago, when washing was done by hand at the nearest stream, monogramming was essential for identifying one neighbor's linen from another's. Today, monogramming is no longer a necessity—but it remains a popular method of personalizing items. Such items might consist of sweatshirts, scarves, pillowcases, towels, pillow shams, checkbook covers, computer mousepads, and more.

General Instructions

One yard of wool Aida will make three scarves.

1. Cut fabric into 10" widths and 70" lengths.
2. Trim all fabric edges along a thread line.
3. Fray the short ends by gently pulling out threads and sewing across the width with thread that matches the fabric color. Optional: Use invisible thread.

4. Fold back the fabric's long ends 1" and press.
5. Fold back ½" again, press under, and sew in hem.
6. Measure up 7" from the bottom of the fringe.
7. Find the center of the scarf and then the center of each half.
8. Using floss or pearl cotton in the color of your choice, stitch letters with the top left letter 10 rows higher than the right letter.

tip

Coordinate color of scarf lettering with color of coat.

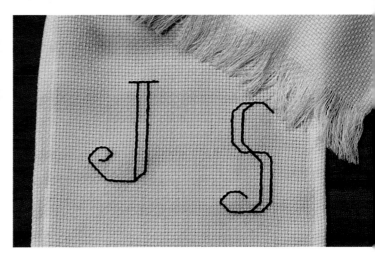

Anchor® 6-Strand Embroidery Floss
403   Black
Anchor® #3 Pearl Cotton
799   Delft Blue, light

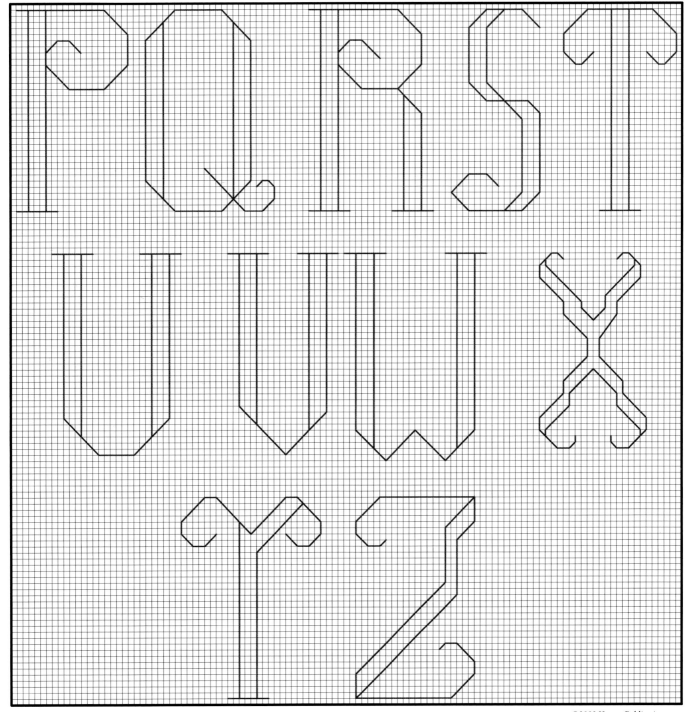

Rose Monogrammed Shirt

Design by Roberta Madeleine
Stitching by Norma Keesler

Add pizzazz to a plain denim shirt with a monogram. Using 10-count waste fabric (canvas) and three strands of floss, stitch one initial centered on a shirt pocket. Backstitch with one strand of floss.

General Instructions

The monogram was taken from the Victorian Rose Alphabet on pages 94 and 95. Instructions for using waste fabric (canvas) are on page 137.

General Instructions

Fabrics

For your first counted cross stitch project, you should choose a fabric with a thread count that you can easily see. Beginners should start with 11- and 14-count fabrics. Six-, 7-, and 8-count fabrics are great for teaching children to cross stitch. As you learn more about counted cross stitch, you can then try finer fabrics that have more threads to the inch. The larger the thread count, the finer the fabric, and thus the more challenging to stitch.

Counted cross stitch is worked on an evenweave fabric that has the same number of threads woven vertically (warp) and horizontally (weft).

Counted thread (cross stitch) means you must count the fabric threads (for linen) or thread squares (for Aida) as you stitch. Evenweave fabrics are available in a variety of colors, fiber content, thread counts, and weave patterns.

Aida is the most popular fabric for cross stitching because of its easy-to-see squares. Aida is woven in a complex weave of groups of four threads that form distinctive squares with corner holes. It is great for beginners. Aida is available in various colors and counts: 6-, 7- (Country Aida), 8-, 10- (primarily damask Aidas), 11-, 14-, 16-, and 18-counts.

Hardanger, available in 100 percent cotton, 100 percent linen, and 100 percent wool, is a 22-count evenweave that can be used for cross stitch as well as hardanger.

Linen is another popular fabric choice for cross stitch. Linen is a plain-weave fabric, which means each fabric thread is woven in the typical over-under method. At the time of this book's production, linen counts ranged from 16-count (from Wichelt Imports) to 55-count (from Zweigart®). Charles Craft has a 20-count linen. The most widely used linen counts are 25-count Dublin, 28-count Cashel, 32-count Belfast, and 36-count Edinburg.

Linen is usually stitched over two threads, although you can stitch over one to achieve even greater detail. When stitching over two threads of the linen (four squares terminology for beginners), the stitch count is half the thread count. For example, if you stitch on 28-count fabric, then 14 cross stitches would encompass 1" of fabric.

Other than linen, there are several plain-weave fabrics that are popular for cross stitching: 28-count Annabelle, 27-count Linda, 28-count Jobelan, and Lugana in 20- (formerly Valerie), 25-, 28- (formerly Brittney), and 32-count.

When cutting fabric, be sure that it is 3" to 4" larger on all sides than the finished design size to allow enough space for matting and other finishing techniques.

Needles

Cross stitch is worked with a tapestry needle that has a blunt tip and a large eye opening to accommodate more threads than a regular sewing needle.

Tapestry needles come in a variety of brands and sizes for use with different fabric counts. See text below for a guide on which to use with each fabric.

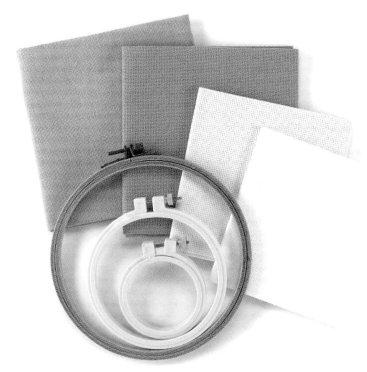

Select a tapestry needle that is small enough not to widen the gap between the fabric threads as you stitch. It also should glide easily through the fabric without piercing or splitting threads.

The following is a basic guide for determining needle size; however, the combination of fabric, number of strands, and type of thread used will be the ultimate guide as to what needle size is the best to flow easily through the fabric.✦

- For 6- and 7-count fabrics, use a size #20 tapestry needle.
- For 8- and 10-count fabrics, use size #22.
- For 11- and 14-count fabrics, use sizes #24 through #26.
- For 16- and 22-count fabrics (32-count over two threads = 16-count), use size #26.
- For 18- and 36-count fabrics (over two threads = 18-count), use sizes #26 through #28.

When embellishing cross stitch with beads, attach beads by using a beading needle that is finer and has a sharp point. If a beading needle is not available, then use an appliqué needle. A size #28 tapestry needle will usually work with the regular seed beads.

Never leave a needle in the design area of fabric, as it will likely leave a rust stain on the fabric or even a hole in the fabric. If storing a needle on the fabric, place it on one of the outer edges that would be in the excess fabric area.

Quick-and-Easy Needle-Threading Technique

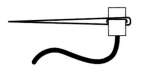

Courtesy Kreinik Mfg. Co.

For a quick-and-easy threading technique, cut a small strip of paper and fold in half. Place the fold through the eye of the needle and open the two ends to insert the thread in between the folded paper. Gently pull the paper through so the thread is brought with it.

Threads

There is a large range of threads available for cross stitching today.

Cotton embroidery floss is the most commonly used thread for counted cross stitch. This floss is 6-stranded and can be divided.

Metallic embroidery floss is a metallic thread to add glitter and sparkle to a project. It is also 6-stranded and divisible.

Rayon floss is a smooth, silky thread with a radiant shine. DMC®'s rayon floss is 6-stranded and Anchor®'s is 4-stranded. This type of floss is slippery and can be difficult to work with because it knots easily. Using shorter strands and moistening the floss with water as you stitch helps to eliminate the kinks. The extra effort in using rayon floss is well worth it because of its beautiful silk-like sheen.

Blending filaments and **metallic threads** are usually combined with other fibers to create sparkling highlights.

Pearl cotton, available in sizes #3 (thickest), #5, #8, and #12 (finest), is twisted, non-separable, and has a lustrous sheen.

Other threads include **silk**, **wool and wool blends**, **Japan thread**, **cord**, **cable**, **silk and metallic ribbon**, **braid**, **over-dyed floss**, and **specialty cottons** such as **Coton 'a Broder**, **flower thread**, and **Floche**.

When working with a piece of

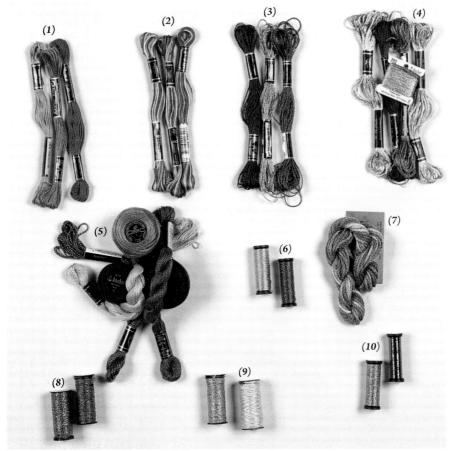

There is an array of threads to choose from. The threads featured above are the most commonly used threads. **1)** Cotton Embroidery Floss **2)** Variegated Floss **3)** Metallic Floss **4)** Rayon Floss **5)** #3, #5, #8, and #12 Pearl Cotton **6)** Silk **7)** Hand-Dyed Floss **8)** Very Fine (#4), Fine (#8), Tapestry (#12), Medium (#16), and Heavy (#32) Braids **9)** ⅛" and ⅟₁₆" Ribbons **10)** Blending Filaments.

cotton floss, cut strands 18" to avoid floss tangling. For metallics and rayons, cut strands 12" to 14" long to prevent fraying and tangling.

For best coverage, separate cotton embroidery floss strands, and then put together the number of strands required for fabric used. Adding strands will create dimension in some designs and other designs will suggest that the number of strands be reduced to create shadows. The basic guidelines for regular counted cross stitch using cotton embroidery/metallic embroidery floss are:

- For 6-, 7-, and 8-count, use six strands.
- For 10- and 11-count, use three to four strands.
- For 14-, 16-, and 18-count, use two strands.
- For 28- and 32-count stitched over two threads, use two strands.

For backstitch, the usual guide is to use one strand (two at the most)—always less than the number of strands used for cross stitch.

Medium (#16) and Heavy (#32) Braids

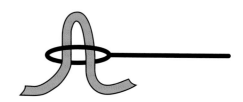

Courtesy Kreinik Mfg. Co.

The medium (#16) and heavy

(#32) braids have a lock-flange mechanism, meaning that the thread "locks" in the groove around the top of the spool. Simply pull the thread to release. Wrap the thread in the groove to secure the unused portion.

Blending Filament

Courtesy Kreinik Mfg. Co.

Blending filament comes on a snap-spool mechanism. Both sides of the spool open; look for the side where the thread end is located. Insert your thumbnail under the cap and rotate the spool while gently lifting the cap to release the thread. (The cap should not pop off.) Snap the lid shut to secure the unused portion.

Blending Filament Threading Technique

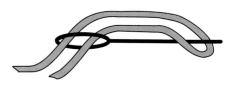

Fold blending filament and thread loop end through needle, as shown above.

Place the loop end over the needle, as shown above.

Slide the loop down to the eye of the needle, forming a slipknot as shown above. Smooth the knot to secure it in place. The knot just formed is small enough to slide through the fabric while allowing you to keep control of your threads. This technique will also make slippery threads stay on the needle without constant rethreading. Then, add regular embroidery floss.

Determining Finished Size

To determine the size of a finished design, divide the stitch count by the number of threads per fabric inch. For example, if a design is 42 stitches wide and 84 stitches high and is stitched on a 14-count fabric, the finished size would be 3" x 6" (42 divided by 14 = 3" and 84 divided by 14 = 6").

If the same project with the same stitch count were stitched on a 28-count fabric over two threads (four squares), the finished size would still be 3" x 6". For designs stitched over two threads, divide the fabric count in half and then divide that number into the stitch count (28 divided by 2 = 14; 42 divided by 14 = 3"; and 84 divided by 14 = 6").

If the same design with the same stitch count were stitched on 28-count over one thread (square), then the finished size would be 1½" x 3", which is determined in the same manner as the first example (42 divided by 28 = 1½" and 84 divided by 28 = 3").

Centering a Design

It is recommended that stitching start from the center point of the chart and fabric. This is the easiest method of assuring accuracy of design placement on the fabric.

To find the center of the fabric, fold the fabric in half horizontally, then vertically. Place a pin in the fold point (or pinch area with fingers) to mark the center.

Then, locate the center of the design on the chart. Most charts will have arrows at top or bottom and along one side. Follow the top arrow down to the center of the chart to square lining up with side arrow.

Cleaning a Stitched Piece

When stitching is done, wash fabric in cold water with a mild soap.

Rinse well and roll the stitched piece in a towel to remove excess water. Do not wring.

Place stitched piece right-side down on a dry towel and iron on warm setting until the stitched fabric is dry.

Treating Stains

If a stitched piece gets a stain, don't panic. Many stains can be removed by following these few simple tips.

First apply a mild soap to the stain and soak in cold water for 15 to 30 minutes.

If a cold-water soak doesn't remove the stain, then treat the stained area with EasyWash®, rub gently, and then soak for about five minutes.

For an especially stubborn stain, the last resort is to try Orvus, which is a safe but strong horse soap. Treat the stained area as you would with the EasyWash®, but since the Orvus is stronger, use it very sparingly. Rinse well with cold water.

Storing a Stitched Piece

Do not store a freshly washed/ironed stitched piece in a plastic bag, as mold will likely occur if the piece is not thoroughly dry. Be sure to let the stitched piece dry thoroughly for two days.

When the piece is completely dry, if possible, store it flat with white towels or white no-acid tissue separating the piece. If unable to store a stitched piece flat, then roll —not fold—the piece and store it.

Be sure to store the piece away from sunlight, as sunlight can fade the colors in the design. Also choose a dry place, as dampness can cause mildew or mold to form on the fabric.

Basic Guidelines of Counted Cross Stitch

Wash your hands before stitching. Do not put hand lotion on before stitching, unless it is Gloves in a Bottle, a special hand lotion for stitchers. See page 141 for details.

When stitching on Aida, an embroidery hoop helps keep the tension consistent. However, the hoop should be removed each time you stop stitching to avoid hoop marks and stubborn creases on the fabric.

If the thread starts to tangle, dangle the needle so that the thread will untwist.

Do not knot the thread, as

knots can create lumps on the front of the piece when it is mounted; can pop through to the front on a loosely woven fabric; can lead to uneven thread tension; and can catch on the floss when stitching.

To avoid thread showing through the front, never carry the thread over more than two or three squares of unstitched fabric.

Work in good light.

Never fold a stitched piece. Always keep it flat or roll it to avoid difficult creases.

Weave ending threads under three to four stitches. Trim excess threads.

Charts

Cross stitch designs are charted on a background of grids. Each square on the chart represents a single cross stitch. There are bold lines every 10 grid squares to make counting quicker and easier. Arrows indicate the center of the design.

Each symbol on the chart represents a different color to be used in that design.

Dark, bold lines represent backstitch lines.

French knots are usually represented by solid large dots.

For the sample chart shown here, there are only full cross stitches and backstitch featured. There are no fractional stitches and no specialty stitches, such as French knots, in this particular design.

When sizes are given for different fabric counts, those are "approximate." For example, this design when stitched on 6-count fabric is "approximately 2⅝" square. The actual size is 2.67" square. The "approximate" size is normally used, rather than the actual size in publishing cross stitch designs. It is for this reason, you need to make certain that you always cut your fabric 3" to 4" larger on all sides than the "approximate" finished size to ensure that you have adequate fabric for matting/framing or whatever finishing technique you prefer.

Project Name: Floral Heart
Designed by Pamela Kellogg
Stitched by Kim Dennett
Stitch count: 16 wide x 16 high

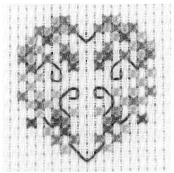

Approximate Finished Sizes	Cross stitch	Backstitch
6-Count: 2⅝" square	6 strands	2 strands
7-Count: 2¼" square	6 strands	2 strands
8-Count: 2" square	4 strands	2 strands
10-Count: 1⅝" square	3 strands	2 strands
11-Count: 1½" square	3 strands	1 strand

Symbol	Floss Brand and Floss Color Number	Floss Color
■	DMC® 320 or Anchor® 215	Pistachio Green, medium
♡	DMC® 368 or Anchor® 214	Pistachio Green, light
★	DMC® 3688 or Anchor® 66	Mauve, medium
m	DMC® 3689 or Anchor® 49	Mauve, light
♥	DMC® 3822 or Anchor® 295	Straw, light

Backstitch Instructions
All backstitch in DMC® 367 or Anchor® 217, Pistachio Green, dark.

Working with Waste Canvas

Waste canvas is used to cross stitch a design onto almost any noneven-weave fabric (i.e. sweatshirt material). Here's how it is done:

1. **Measure** the garment front or the area to be stitched and compare the measurements to those of the charted design. Cut the waste canvas 2" to 3" larger than the design on all sides. Bind the edges of the canvas with masking tape to prevent the raw edges from snagging the garment fabric.

2. **Center** the waste canvas on the area to be stitched. The blue lines should run horizontally or vertically with the weave of the fabric to ensure that the stitched design will be straight.

3. **Basting:** To prevent the waste canvas from slipping while the design is being stitched, it is necessary to baste the waste fabric securely to the garment on all four sides, as well as diagonally, and from side to side. For larger designs, extra lines of basting may be necessary to further secure the waste canvas in place. These lines also help in centering your design.

4. **Stitching your design:** Beginning in the center, work the design in cross stitch by stitching through the canvas and the garment fabric just the way you would normally stitch on Aida fabric. Be very careful not to puncture the canvas threads. Pierced threads

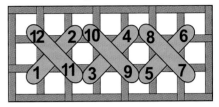

Waste canvas instructions courtesy of Charles Craft, Inc. Charles Craft's waste fabric (canvas) is available in three count sizes: 8.5, 10, and 14.

can be difficult to remove later. Follow the chart and color key legend of your charted design. It is suggested to use three strands for cross stitch and two for backstitch on 8.5-count canvas, and two for cross stitch and one for backstitch on 14-count canvas.

5. **Removing waste canvas threads:** Once all stitching is complete, remove all basting stitches and trim waste canvas to within 1" of the stitched area on all sides. Dampen the waste canvas threads until they become limp. Pull out the canvas threads one at a time, using tweezers, if necessary. Be sure to pull the threads low to the fabric. Only pull in the direction of the canvas threads. Do not pull up or at an angle. Damp threads will snap or break if pulled incorrectly. To make removal of long threads easier, when working large designs, it may be helpful to cut the waste canvas threads between areas of stitching.

6. **Laundering:** Launder by hand only with mild liquid soap. Roll garment in a towel to remove excess water. Air dry flat. If ironing is necessary, press using a pressing cloth on the wrong side of the garment. Iron should be set on a medium heat setting.

Stitch Diagrams

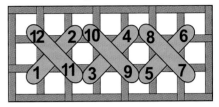

Cross Stitch

It is important that all your stitches lay in the same direction for a better overall finish/look of your project. Bottom stitches go from the bottom left corner to the upper right corner; top stitches from the bottom right corner to the upper left corner. Make all the bottom stitches in a row, working from left to right, then cross them as you work back from right to left.

Number 1 in the figure is the starting point of the first bottom stitch. Come up at 1, down at 2, up at 3, down at 4, up at 5, down at 6. Each stitch on the bottom row represents a half-stitch.

Number 7 is the starting point of your top stitches—completing the stitches. Go up at 7, down at 8, up at 9, down at 10, up at 11, down at 12. The stitches are now full cross stitches.

Backstitch

Backstitch is used for outlining, lettering, and other design lines. Unless the directions state differently for a certain project, you usually backstitch with one strand (two at the most)—generally less than the number of strands used for cross stitch.

Pull the needle through at 1, go down at 2, up at 3, down at 4, up at 5, down at 6. Continue with the forward-two-stitches, back-one-stitch pattern.

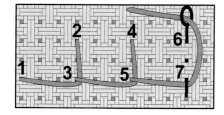

Blanket Stitch

Come up at 1 at edge of fabric. Go down at 2 about ¼" away, come back up at 3 behind the thread, down at 4, and up at 5. Pull the thread to remove any slack, but not enough to distort the stitch. For the bear vest featured in this book, there are three rows of stitches between each stitch and three rows wide.

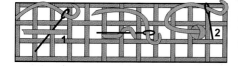

French Knot

French knots are usually indicated by a solid dot on a chart. Use one strand of floss and bring the needle up at 1. Wrap the needle two times with the floss. Hold the floss tightly as you insert the needle back into the fabric near the same place.

At 2 on the figure, pull needle through to form a small knot on top of the fabric.

Note: Some designs will deviate from the usual one strand wrapped twice to achieve greater dimension. In those cases, follow the instructions provided for that particular design using the same technique as above.

Substituting Beads for French Knots

In most designs where French knots are featured, you can substitute beads in place of the knots if you desire. Choose a bead color to match the floss color called for in the French knots.

Attaching Beads

There are several methods for attaching beads that ensure all beads are facing the same direction without tilting—vertically, horizontally, or diagonally. I prefer the Half Cross Stitch, followed by the horizontal technique. These two tend to be more secure and more pleasing to stitch than the other two methods. I suggest you experiment with all techniques on a scrap piece of fabric. Then proceed with your project, using the technique that you are most comfortable with.

Half Cross Stitch

Beginning in the lower left corner of the thread intersection, come

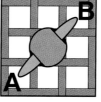

(Bead openings going from bottom left corner to top right corner.)

up at A, attach a bead, and go down at B in the upper right corner of the intersection. Go back through the bead from A to B to ensure that the bead is secure. Using a half cross stitch to attach beads is the most popular technique because it is the easiest and fastest. However, with this method, the beads can have a tendency to tilt/move. The half cross stitch reinforced is still my preference with the horizontal technique as second.

Diagonal Bead

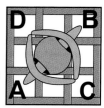

From the back of the fabric, come up at A, stitch through the bead, go down at B, come up at C, and go down at D, separating the floss

(Bead openings going from bottom left corner to top right corner.)

strands so that one strand lays on each side of the bead. Tighten the thread tension to hold the bead in place.

Vertical Bead

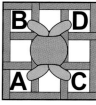

From the back of the fabric, come up at A, stitch through the bead, go down at B, come up at C, enter from the A-

(Bead openings going up and down.)

side of the bead to make it vertical, and then go back down at D.

Horizontal Bead

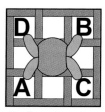

From the back of the fabric, come up at A, stitch through the bead, go down at B, come up at C, enter from

(Bead openings going from side to side.)

the B-side of the bead to make it horizontal, and then go back down at D.

Needlework Accessories

Today, needlework accessories are customized for cross stitchers. Those featured in this section are some of the most important to start with. While all the products make stitching more fun, some are vital to what I call "good-sense stitching."

Take special care of your eyes and stitching hands to ensure many years of stitching for the future.

Wrist Support Glove

Thera-Glove™ makes a fingerless, stretchy support glove that has a wide wristband to help keep your wrists straight, helping to avoid carpal tunnel syndrome.

Lighting/Magnification

It is crucial to work in good lighting. OTT-LITE® is one of several manu-facturers of light and magnifier products. The model shown is OTT-LITE® TrueColor™ Floor Lamp with Optional Magnifier attachment. OTT-LITE® lamps have a "natural daylight" feature with low glare and low heat. The optional magnifier with a flexible neck has a wide field of view and extends to about 24" from the lamp.

Needle Organizers

DMC®'s needle organizer has five compartments. The clear snap-top lid keeps the needles within view, while holding them securely inside.

LoRan® has a magnetic needle case with a clear plastic Snap-Lock™ top for security. The back can attach to LoRan®'s magnet board for easy access.

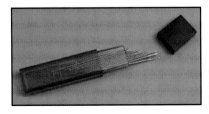

Needle Threaders

LoRan®'s needle threader has an exclusive Needle-Notch™ to hold the needle while threading and the Shoulder-Stop™ design stops the needle at the proper location.

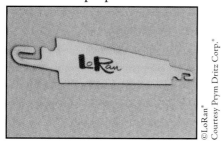

1. Hang the needle on the threader, as shown below.

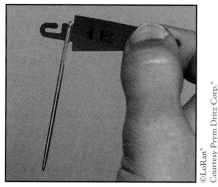

2. Lay the floss/yarn over the hook, as shown below.

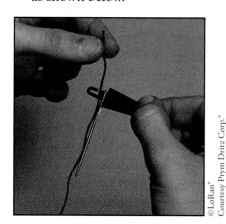

3. Pull the thread through the threader, as shown.

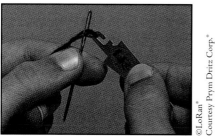

DMC®'s needle threader works with three thread weights. One hook threads heavy-weight, one medium-weight, and a wire is for fine threads. It also accommodates short- and long-eye needles.

1. Hold the threader to the needle eye, as shown at left.

2. Place the threader through the needle eye and hook the thread, as shown below.

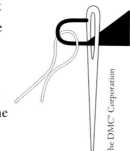

3. Pull the thread back through the needle eye with the threader, as shown in the illustration below.

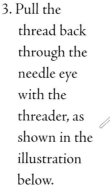

Floss/Thread Organizers

DMC® has a new floss organizer in a distinctive horse head-shaped plastic. It holds up to 14 floss colors.

LoRan®'s project cards come in two sizes. The small card holds nine floss colors, the large 20. Each card has a magnetic strip at the top for a needle. They also have areas for identifying floss color numbers.

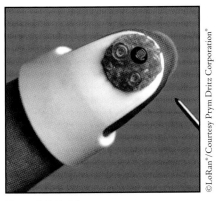

Bead Nabber

LoRan®'s bead nabber adjusts to any finger size. The nabber holds beads for easy threading and helps eliminate skewering beads. It further protects fingers from the tip of the needle.

Magnetic Boards

Magnetic boards by LoRan®, shown below, are available in several sizes: 12" x 18", 6" x 10", and 8" x 10". They are my favorite needlework accessories. These boards hold your charts in place with additional magnetic strips. You can also use LoRan's line magnifier with these boards.

Twin Pointed Quick-Stitch Needles

John James' Twin Pointed Quick-Stitch Needles have rounded tapestry points on both ends with one long and narrow eye in the center. The needles come in sizes #20, #22, #24, #26, and #28. There is no turning with these needles, so you drop the needle fewer times. This type of needle not only makes stitching faster, but also helps reduce the carpal tunnel syndrome threat.

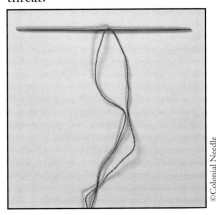

Using a hands-free frame, keep one hand above your work and one below. Stitch straight up and down through your fabric without turning the needle around, looping the thread over a finger to keep it taut and prevent twisting. Hold the needle close to the eye.

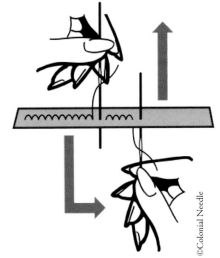

Lotion for Needleworkers

Natural oils from our hands can be a problem when the oils leave a residue on fabric. Many stitchers try to use a conventional hand lotion, thinking it will resolve the problem ... but in the long run, it only complicates the problem. Therefore, stitchers are usually cautioned not to apply lotion to their hands prior to stitching because the lotion will rub off onto the fabric.

Gloves In A Bottle, however, claims its lotion "turns your outer layer of skin into what works like an invisible pair of gloves to keep the moisture-robbing irritants out while retaining your own natural moisture. The lotion lasts four hours or more, and comes off naturally with exfoliated skin cells. It does not come off when you wash or touch something." The company further states: "It (the lotion) prevents the hands' natural oils from getting onto fine fabrics and threads, keeping your work cleaner."

I've used this lotion with great success.

Embroidery Floss Conversion Chart

This chart should be used only as a guide. It is difficult to give exact alternatives between brands since color comparisons are subject to personal preference. Conversions are given for a total of 450 solid colors in the following brands: Anchor® and DMC®.

DMC	ANCHOR	DMC	ANCHOR	DMC	ANCHOR	DMC	ANCHOR	DMC	ANCHOR	DMC	ANCHOR
White	2	422	943	721	925	869	944	3012	844	3779	1012
Ecru	387	433	358	722	323	890	218	3013	842	3781	904
150	59	434	310	725	305	891	35	3021	905	3782	899
151	73	435	1046	726	295	892	33	3022	8581	3787	273
152	969	436	1045	727	293	893	28	3023	1040	3790	393
153	95	437	362	728	305	894	27	3024	397	3799	236
154	873	444	290	729	890	895	1044	3031	905	3801	1098
155	1030	445	288	730	845	898	360	3032	903	3802	1019
156	118	451	233	732	281	899	52	3033	391	3803	972
157	120	452	676	733	280	900	333	3041	871	3804	63
158	178	453	231	734	279	902	897	3042	870	3805	62
159	120	469	267	738	372	904	258	3045	888	3806	62
160	175	470	267	739	387	905	257	3046	945	3807	122
161	176	471	266	740	316	906	256	3047	852	3808	1068
162	159	472	253	741	304	907	255	3051	681	3809	1066
163	877	498	1005	742	303	909	923	3052	262	3810	1066
164	240	500	683	743	302	910	229	3053	261	3811	1060
165	278	501	878	744	301	911	205	3064	883	3812	188
166	280	502	877	745	300	912	209	3072	847	3813	875
167	374	503	876	746	275	913	204	3078	292	3814	1074
168	234	505	210	747	158	915	1029	3325	129	3815	877
169	235	517	162	754	1012	917	89	3326	36	3816	876
208	110	518	1039	758	9575	918	341	3328	1024	3817	875
209	109	519	1038	760	1022	919	340	3340	329	3818	923
210	108	520	862	761	1021	920	1004	3341	328	3819	278
211	342	522	860	762	234	921	1003	3345	268	3820	306
221	897	523	859	772	259	922	1003	3346	267	3821	305
223	895	524	858	775	128	924	840	3347	266	3822	295
224	893	535	401	777	65	926	838	3348	264	3823	386
225	1026	543	933	778	968	927	837	3350	59	3824	8
300	352	550	102	779	380	928	847	3354	74	3825	323
301	1049	552	99	780	309	930	1035	3362	263	3826	1049
304	1006	553	98	782	308	931	1034	3363	262	3827	311
307	289	554	96	783	307	932	1033	3364	260	3828	373
309	42	561	212	791	178	934	862	3371	382	3829	901
310	403	562	210	792	941	935	269	3607	87	3830	5975
311	148	563	208	793	176	936	269	3608	86	3831	29
312	979	564	206	794	175	937	268	3609	85	3832	28
315	1019	580	281	796	133	938	381	3685	1028	3833	26
316	1017	581	280	797	132	939	152	3687	68	3834	100
317	400	597	1064	798	131	943	188	3688	66	3835	98
318	399	598	1062	799	136	945	881	3689	49	3836	90
319	218	600	59	800	144	946	332	3705	35	3837	100
320	215	601	57	801	359	947	330	3706	33	3838	177
321	9046	602	63	803	149	948	1011	3708	31	3839	176
322	978	603	62	807	168	950	4146	3712	1023	3840	117
326	59	604	55	809	130	951	1010	3713	1020	3841	9159
327	100	605	1094	813	161	954	203	3716	25	3842	164
333	119	606	334	814	45	955	206	3721	896	3843	1089
334	977	608	332	815	44	956	41	3722	1027	3844	410
335	38	610	889	816	1005	957	50	3726	1018	3845	1089
336	150	611	898	817	13	958	187	3727	1016	3846	1090
340	118	612	832	818	23	959	186	3731	76	3847	1076
341	117	613	831	819	271	961	76	3733	75	3848	1074
347	1025	632	936	820	134	962	75	3740	872	3849	1070
349	13	640	903	822	390	963	73	3743	869	3850	189
350	11	642	392	823	152	964	185	3746	1030	3851	187
351	10	644	830	824	164	966	206	3747	120	3852	306
352	9	645	273	825	162	967	6	3750	1036	3853	1003
353	6	646	8581	826	161	970	316	3752	1032	3854	313
355	1014	647	1040	827	160	972	298	3753	1031	3855	311
356	5975	648	900	828	9159	973	297	3755	140	3856	1010
367	217	666	46	829	906	975	355	3756	1037	3857	936
368	214	676	891	830	277	976	1001	3760	169	3858	1007
369	1043	677	956	831	277	977	1002	3761	928	3859	914
370	855	680	901	832	907	986	246	3765	170	3860	678
371	854	699	923	833	907	987	244	3766	167	3861	677
372	853	700	228	834	874	988	243	3768	779	3862	358
400	351	701	227	837	927	989	242	3770	1009	3863	379
402	1047	702	226	838	1088	991	1076	3771	336	3864	376
407	914	703	238	839	1086	992	1072	3772	1007	3865	2
413	236	704	256	840	1084	993	1070	3774	778	3866	926
414	235	712	926	841	1082	995	410	3776	1048	B5200	1
415	398	718	88	842	1080	996	433	3777	1015		
420	375	720	326	844	1041	3011	846	3778	1013		

Resources

Adam Original
Phone: (763) 425-7843
Web site: www.adamoriginal.com
11-count Antique White Pearl Aida
Album Cover (page 90); 10-count
Navy Blue Tula Checkbook Cover
(page 54); Tree Skirt (page 41); Tula
Pillow Shams with Ruffled Trim (page
70); 7-count White Klostern Stocking
(page 36); 7-count Sand Klostern
Stocking (page 33); 10-count Sand
Tula Bear Vest (page 39); and 7-count
Sand and 7-count Cream Klostern
Adult Vests (page 125).

Charles Craft, Inc.
Phone: (800) 277-0980
Web site: www.charlescraft.com
7-count White Monk's Cloth (page
23); 11-count White Aida (page 116);
and 8.5-count Waste Canvas (page
131).

Coats & Clark, Inc.
Phone: (704) 329-5016
Web site: www.coatsandclark.com
Anchor® 6-Strand Embroidery Floss,
Anchor® Pearl Cotton #3, and Anchor®
Variegated Embroidery Floss.
Mail-order source for Anchor:
Herrschners, Inc. (800) 441-0838.

Colonial Needle, Inc.
Phone: (914) 237-6434
Web site: www.colonialneedle.com
Twin Pointed Quick-Stitch Needles
(page 141).

Daniel Enterprises, Inc.
Phone: (910) 270-9090
Web site: www.crafterspride.com
Acrylic Coasters (page 86).

The DMC® Corporation
Web site: www.dmc-usa.com
DMC® 6-Strand Embroidery Floss;
DMC® 6-Strand Rayon Floss;
DMC® 6-Strand Metallic Floss;
DMC® Metallic Thread; DMC® Pearl
Cotton #3; 11-count White Aida
(pages 29, 37, 64, 71, 86, 88, 93, and
98); Floss Organizer (page 140); and
Needle Organizers (page 139).
Mail-order source for DMC®
Corporation: Herrschners, Inc.
(800) 441-0838.

Gay Bowles Sales, Inc.
Phone: (608) 754-9466
Web site: www.millhill.com
Pebble Beads (page 39) and Star Glass
Treasures (pages 39 and 116).

Gloves In A Bottle, Inc.
Phone: (818) 248-9980
Web site: www.glovesinabottle.com
Lotion (page 141).

Kreinik Mfg. Co.
Phone: (410) 281-0040
Web site: www.kreinik.com
Kreinik braids, Kreinik ribbons, and
Kreinik blending filaments (page 41).

LoRan®/Dal-Craft, Inc.
Phone: (770) 939-2894
Web site: www.lorancrafts.com
Bead Nabber and Magnetic Board
(page 141), Project Cards (page 140),
Needle Case (page 139), and Needle
Threader (page 140).

Ott-Lite® Technology
Phone: (800) 842-8848
Web site: www.ott-lite.com
Lights and magnifiers (page 139).

Sudberry House
Phone: (860) 739-6951
Web site: www.sudberry.com
Small Tea Tray #80031 (page 88).

Thera-Glove Products
Phone: (845) 534-9087
Web site: www.thera-glove.com
Thera-Glove™ (page 141).

X-Stitch Enterprises
Phone: (512) 251-3306
Web site: www.x-stitchenterprises.com
7-count Black Country Aida Table
Topper (page 119); 7-count Black
Country Aida Shawl (page 122);
10-count Eggshell Ring Bearer's Pillow
(page 15); 10-count Eggshell Bride's
Purse (page 15); and 10-count White
Tula Pillow Sham (page 49).

Zweigart® THE needlework fabric™
Phone: (732) 562-8888
Web site: www.zweigart.com
8-count White Cottage Huck Towels
(pages 80-85); 8-count White Cottage
Huck Bib and Towel (page 26);
10-count Cream Candle Doilies/
Mini Tabletop Tree Skirts (page 55);
10-count Gold/Cream Metallic Rondo
Table Toppers (pages 11 and 44);
10-count White Rondo Table Topper
(page 14); 10-count white and Delft
Blue Octav Table Toppers (page 67);
10-count Seafoam Green Rondo Table
Topper (page 18); 10-count Largo
Table Topper (page 113); 11-count
Beige Aida (page 110); 10-count
Antique White Merino Afghan (page
97); and 11-count White Wool Aida
(page 129).
Mail-order source for Zweigart® items:
Needleworker's Delight
(800) 931-4545.

Contributing Designers

The beautiful projects featured in this book are works from the following creative designers.

Phyllis Dobbs
25th Wedding Anniversary Table Topper (page 11)
50th Wedding Anniversary Table Topper (page 11)
Ring Bearer's Pillow and Bridal Purse (page 15)
Wedding Table Topper (page 18)
Festive Bear's Vest (page 39)
Happy Birthday Table Topper (page 113)

Pam Kellogg
Baby Bib and Towel Set (page 26)
Four Seasons Candle Doilies (page 55)
Rejoice in the Lord Framed Piece (page 64)
Cottage Huck Fruit Towels (page 80)
Our Family Memories Album Cover (page 90)
Morning Glories Vests (page 125)
Floral Heart (page 136)

Roberta Madeleine
Baby Birth Announcement (page 29)
Daisy Checkbook Cover (page 54)
Four Seasons Coasters (page 86)
Teatime Tray (page 88)
Victorian Rose Alphabet (page 93)
The Path Sampler (page 110)
Graduation Sampler (page 116)
Hawaiian Floral Shawl (page 122)
Monogrammed Denim Shirt (page 131)
BJ's Signature Logo (back cover)

Anne Stanton
Blending Filament Threading Diagram (page 134)
Cross Stitch Diagram (page 137)
Backstitch Diagram (page 137)
Waste Canvas Diagram (page 137)
French Knot Diagram (page 138)
Bead Diagrams (page 138)
Blanket Stitch Diagram (page 138)

Mike Vickery
Moose Stocking (page 33)
Ornament Stocking (page 36)
Ornament Tree Skirt (page 41)
Poinsettia Table Topper (page 44)
Daisy Pillow Sham (page 49)
Rhode Island Red Rooster and Buff Orpington
Hen Pillow Shams and Framed Pieces (page 70)
Flowers in the Garden of Life
Afghan and Framed Verse (page 97)
Halloween Bear Table Topper (page 119)
Winter Scarf (page 128)